THE SEVEN CHURCHES OF ASIA MINOR

•THE CHURCHES IN REVELATION•

DR. ORVILLE R. BECKFORD SR.

THE SEVEN CHURCHES OF ASIA MINOR:
THE CHURCHES IN REVELATION
Copyright © 2018 by Dr. Orville R. Beckford Sr.

All rights reserved. No part of this publication may be reproduced, distributed, or transmitted in any form or by any means, including photocopying, recording, or other electronic or mechanical methods, without the prior written permission of the publisher or author, except in the case of brief quotations embodied in critical reviews and certain other noncommercial uses permitted by copyright law.

Although every precaution has been taken to verify the accuracy of the information contained herein, the author and publisher assume no responsibility for any errors or omissions. No liability is assumed for damages that may result from the use of information contained within.

Because of the dynamic nature of the Internet, any web addresses or links contained in this book may have changed since publication and may no longer be valid. The views expressed in this work are solely those of the author and do not necessarily reflect the views of the publisher, and the publisher hereby disclaims any responsibility for them.

All Scripture references are taken from the King James Version (KJV) unless where otherwise indicated.

Other references are found in the Good News Translation (GNT) from Biblegateway copyright 1992 by American Bible Society.

English Standard Version (ESV) Biblegateway, Copyright 2001 by Crossway Bibles, a division of Good News Publishers

GOD'S WORD Translation (GW) Biblegateway, Copyright 1995 by God's Word to the Nations.

Amplified Bible (AMP) Biblegateway, Copyright 1954, 1958, 1962, 1964, 1965, 1987, by the Lockman Foundation.

Library of Congress Control Number:	2018963691
ISBN-13: Paperback:	978-1-64398-500-8
PDF:	978-1-64398-501-5
ePub:	978-1-64398-502-2
Kindle:	978-1-64398-503-9
Hardcover:	978-1-64398-504-6

Printed in the United States of America

LitFire LLC
1-800-511-9787
www.litfirepublishing.com
order@litfirepublishing.com

The Seven Churches of Asia Minor: The Churches in Revelation
by Dr. Orville R. Beckford, Sr.

LitFire Publishing

Book review by Donna Ford

"[John] was one of Jesus' closest friends. But none of his past experiences with Christ prepared him for this moment."

Students of Revelation—the final book of the Bible—are familiar with the letters Christ gave to the seven churches of Asia Minor as recorded by the Apostle John. At the time of this vision, John was exiled on the nearby island of Patmos. Some dispensational Bible scholars believe these church letters represent the history of the Church from 30-100 AD and 1960-present times. The angels mentioned may have been real people, responsible as lights to pass on Christianity to their church members. Beckford includes in each chapter information about the location of the church mentioned in Revelation, the glorified Christ's introduction, Jesus' critique with specific mention of each church's works with a promise/warning to believers. and the author's application for today's churches.

For example, Pergamos was the third church to receive a letter from Christ. Prominent when Alexander the Great controlled Pergamum, this city became the home of many religions and false doctrines. Christ appears having a two-edged sword (his Word) and promises a white stone for those who overcome. The author uses excerpts from the Old Testament, the Gospels, and the Epistles to explain the symbolism.

Beckford has produced a scholarly addition to books already written about the seven churches of Asia. A major contribution of this in-depth commentary is the gathering in one location of references from well-known Bible scholars including William Barclay, Matthew Henry, Finis Dake, and David Guzik. The included pronunciation of the Greek words is helpful, but also featuring the word's Anglicized spelling would have been useful. The author provides helpful background and maps showing these seven actual churches situated in the shape of a horseshoe at the western end of Asia Minor. Students of the Bible may find this work a useful addition to their library.

ENDORSEMENTS

Dr. Beckford's book is a comprehensive and thoughtful study of the seven churches of Asia Minor and their historical and prophetic significance. His extensive focus on the Laodicean church, ascribing it to today's lukewarm church, should serve as a wake-up call to every modern-day pastor.

Dr. Neil Weaver
President
Louisiana Baptist University & Theological Seminary
Shreveport LA

Beckford was my student for four years and my friend for many more. Dr. Beckford and his wife ministered in our church in praise, worship, and the Word. He pastored several miles from the church I pastored but close enough to view his work and ministry. Among the many good things that I could say about him, he was always willing to tackle any challenge put before him, and he always worked to make himself a better Christian, student, pastor, and friend. His work on *The Seven Churches of Asia Minor* is a testimony to his spirit and desire. The work shows his academic interest and abilities. He was always sure he could do more to make a positive difference in his life and the lives of others. Congratulations on another fine achievement!

Pastor George Grace
Senior Pastor, First Bible Baptist Church
Rochester NY

This offering by Dr. Orville Beckford, Sr., *The Seven Churches of Asia Minor: Their Location, Characteristics, and Christ Introducing Himself to Them in Seven Different Ways*, is an attempt to enlighten the heart, mind, and spirit of each reader to the ministry of Christ to the seven churches of Asia Minor. This work will serve as reminder to us today that as the head of the church, Christ alone speaks words of warning, counsel, and blessing to his body on earth.

Cervin L. McKinnon
Regional Presiding Bishop
Church of God of Prophecy
Northeast Region USA & Bermuda

Dr. Beckford has done an utterly fascinating treatment of the subject. A wonderful and unique read for the Christian faith. I highly recommend this book to all believers.

Bishop Fetson S. Leak
Presiding Prelate
Church of Deliverance Ministries

I have known Dr. Orville Beckford for over fifteen years and have observed him as a student, pastor, teacher, preacher, author, and friend. He has excelled at each of these positions and displayed an impeccable character. I endorse him in this endeavor to write on the seven churches of Asia Minor in Revelation. I know he will edify, encourage, and challenge all of us in our faith.

Dr. Robert Brado
Pastor, Faith Bible Church
Rochester NY

An insightful pastoral treatment of the seven churches of Revelation by an experienced pastor. Readers who have been intimidated by this challenging portion of the Scriptures will benefit from Dr. Beckford's research and applications.

Bishop Earl W. McKay
District Overseer, Bronx Manhattan & Bermuda District, COGOP

Dr. Beckford's book on The Seven Churches of Revelation is a highly recommended book for today's student of the Bible. It is superbly researched and appropriately challenges the validity of the vast number of prophets and prophecies flowing in our churches today. As a student of the word of God, I concur with the author.

Bishop Martin Nelson
Senior Pastor of Bezer Holiness Church
New Rochelle, New York

With deep love, appreciation, and fond memories to my mother,

Ivy Mae Henry

Who brought me into this world, nurtured, guided, and greatly influenced my life in ways more than I can say in few words. She has done a lot to shape my life in the absence of my deceased father; guided me socially, and greatly impacted my walk with, and service to the Lord. She paved the way for me to enter into church leadership, that eventually lead to full-time pastoral ministry. Her time on earth, and decades of dedicated work and service to the Lord has ended, but the impact and influence she had and still have on her children, grandchildren, family and friends near and far, will live forever. My mother was a source of strength, and one who looked out for the wellbeing of her family physically, emotionally, and spiritually. Memories don't leave like people do they will always stay with you, and that is the truism of her life and memory. Gone but will never be forgotten, her legacy lives on!

This book will bring to light the reasons behind Christ's letters to the seven churches, and why he introduced himself to each one of them in a different way. It will be a great eye opener to the minds of those who crave knowledge. There's a lot to understand about these churches in history, and what lessons one should learn by comparing these churches to the church today.

Many have just read the text on these seven churches, but few have taken the time to evaluate their significance. By God's grace and the work of the Holy Spirit guiding you into all truth, you will leave with a much better understanding, and a desire for more.

PERGAMUM
The lax and compromising church

THYATIRA
The loose compromising church of the dark ages

SMYRNA
The loyal church that suffers martyrdom

SARDIS
The lifeless church with a name
That it is alive

EPHESUS
The lacking church that left its first love

PHILADELPHIA
The loving church with an open door

LAODICEA
The Lukewarm church, materially rich,
but spiritually poor

THE APPROXIMATE PERIODS OF THE CHURCHES

Ephesus (Rev. 2:1-7) **(30-100 AD)** The First Century Apostolic Church.

Smyrna (Rev. 2:8-11) **(100-313 AD)** The Age of Roman Persecution

Pergamum (Rev.2:12-17) **(313-600 AD)** The Age of Constantine

Thyatira (Rev. 2:18-29) **(600-1517 AD)** The Dark Ages

Sardis (Rev. 3:1-6) **(1517-1648 AD)** The Protestant Reformation

Philadelphia (Rev. 3:7-13) **(1648-1900s AD)** The missionary Movement

Laodicea (Rev. 3:14-22) **(1960-Present)** The Age of Apostasy Leading to Christ's Return

CONTENTS

Foreword xvii
Preface xix
Introduction xxi

Chapter 1   The Seven Churches' Geographical Location 1
Chapter 2   The Revelation of Jesus Christ 8
Chapter 3   Ephesus 20
Chapter 4   The Church of Ephesus 30
Chapter 5   The Church of Smyrna 54
Chapter 6   The Church of Pergamos 73
Chapter 7   The Church of Thyatira 83
Chapter 8   The Church of Sardis 95

Chapter 9   The Church of Philadelphia........................ 114
Chapter 10 The Church of Laodicea............................ 132
Chapter 11 THE GLORY SHALL RETURN TO THE CHURCH ... 150

Conclusion... 169
Bibliography 190
ABOUT THE AUTHOR....................................... 195

FOREWORD

Before the great apostle John came to the end of his earthly sojourn, having outlived the other original apostles, he was chosen to write yet another book that would come to be a part of the New Testament. Whereas his gospel was a treatise on the life and ministry of our Lord that culminated in His death, burial, and resurrection, this new task addressed things yet future. It would be called the unveiling, or the revelation, of Jesus. Christ.

The book actually began as a letter written to seven churches that existed near the end of the first century AD. In it, the Lord addressed both their strengths and weaknesses. The author of the book you are holding has explored these seven letters diligently. This book, the result of his research, is a significant contribution to understanding what the Lord had to say to these churches nearly two thousand years ago as well as to His people today.

It has been my privilege to serve as the dean of biblical studies here at Louisiana Baptist University during the time that Dr. Beckford was preparing this work.

David A. Keeny
Dean of Biblical Studies
Shreveport LA

PREFACE

The seven churches of Asia Minor mentioned in Revelation 2–3 have always interested me, causing me to want to learn more about them, their importance, and what should be learned from them. This initiated the desire to write this dissertation on those churches with the hope of finding out some things that were unique about them.

This book intends to take a look at these churches from their historical, geographical, and ecclesiastical backgrounds. It is my wish that this will help readers better understand their significance in the life of the church and how each one represents a time (not only for historical purposes) in the dispensation of the church—the body of Christ.

This book will look at why Christ introduced himself in seven different ways to each of these churches. For those who have not taken the time to study them, it is hoped that this dissertation will bring to light the struggles they faced and how they dealt with heresy, adversity, immorality, persecution, and even martyrdom. There are many lessons to be learned from these seven churches that will be an eye-opener to all Christians individually and to churches corporately. All of the churches will be looked at individually but greater emphasis will be placed on the Laodicean church, as it represents the current age and status of the church, based on the letter it received.

Let me take this time to say thanks to the Lord who has given me the strength, the desire for knowledge, and the passion to pursue this finding. To him be all the glory, majesty, and power. Special thanks to my wife, Deana, for bearing with and supporting me through this long and hard road of reading, researching, and writing. It has been many months of long days and nights of separation and loneliness, but through it all, she stood with me in prayer and encouraged me to keep going, although sometimes it looked unlikely to be accomplished. Thanks also to the members and friends of GNLC who have continued to pray for me and had the spirit of motivation, anticipating a successful end to the process.

INTRODUCTION

The seven churches of Asia Minor mentioned by Christ in Revelation are fascinating and intriguing to say the least. It is interesting to observe how they fit characteristically throughout the ages, though they were real churches literally located in areas mentioned by Christ. It should also be noted that there were not just seven churches within the demographics mentioned; however, seven were chosen apparently because of their individual experiences or character and what they portrayed that would be significant throughout the life of the church on earth.

The observation of their experiences show that it is not by chance that these seven churches were chosen. In keeping with God's principle of the number seven as the number of completion or perfection, it makes sense that there were seven churches, not nine or ten, let alone six, the number of man.

As a good look is taken at these churches, an attempt will be made to delve into the historical facts of their existence, the prophetic accuracy of Christ's message, and how they have been fulfilled throughout the ages.

Most people can only truly testify of the seventh church (although many commentators and theologians believe all of the characteristics of the churches existed through all ages, and still exist), which is the Laodicean church. However, as one takes a deeper look at the historical writings of the patriarchs who have put an enormous amount of time studying these churches by eras and observing their personal testimonies of the realities of their time, he or she will see the things the churches faced while others could only speak of what the church is experiencing today as current fulfillment.

For those privileged to read this writing, he or she will also be able to identify with these truths and compare the church then and now. Based on the fulfillments that can be seen today, it proves that these are indeed the last of the last days, which puts the church definitely in the Laodicean age, and when it is observed carefully, it makes it clear that this must be the epitome of the church throughout the ages.

One would think that based on Jesus' warnings in these letters and his admonition to all who hear to take heed, it would create a sense of urgency that would propel preachers, teachers, and church leaders to place great emphasis on the subject. "He that hath an ear, let him hear what the Spirit saith unto the churches" (Revelation 2:7). More attention need to be given by leaders to avoid these detrimental mistakes that were made by these churches and be better prepared for the challenges the church will face. Jesus warned these churches, particularly the Laodicean church (believed without a doubt that it's where the church is now), but it seems to have no effect on how the church is influenced today by the way it conducts itself.

It is inconceivable that preachers and pastors are not more careful to avoid falling into the same trap of putting material gain over spiritual development. It is said that those who do not learn from history are destined to repeat it. It appears, however, that the hardest thing for people to do, on a general basis, is to learn from others' failures or mistakes. The apostle Paul mentioned in Hebrews 4:2, "For unto us was the gospel preached, as well as unto them: but the word preached did not profit them, not being mixed with faith in them that heard it."

This is an indictment against the last-days church leaders who fail to recognize the times and season of the church in history. If leaders are cognizant of this letter and are influenced by the Holy Spirit, they would not allow God's house to be dominated and manipulated by materialistic cravings and the greed for monetary gain and, by this, not recognizing the absence of the manifestation of the Holy Spirit in the churches. The awareness of and submission to the Holy Spirit's presence will influence what is preached and taught.

Today it is difficult (and in some cases impossible) to differentiate between the church and the world based on how some churches operate like social gatherings. This is not a new phenomenon, unfortunately, but past experiences and consequences should help shape the way those who desire the coveted position of church leadership will conduct themselves and avoid these pitfalls.

It is beyond comprehension that preachers could become so blinded and oblivious to the prophetic teachings of Christ and the apostles that they pay no real attention to what Christ actually stated in his letters to these churches. There are very few differences between the church and the world; in too many instances, the same can be seen happening where the church sometimes look like the world based on what takes priority in the life and function of many churches today.

Another thing that needs attention is what Paul calls "not enduring sound doctrine." Preachers are admonished to

> Preach the word; be instant in season, out of season; reprove, rebuke, exhort with all longsuffering and doctrine. For the time will come when they will not endure sound doctrine; but

after their own lusts shall they heap to themselves teachers, having itching ears; and they shall turn away their ears from the truth, and shall be turned unto fables. (2 Timothy 4:2–4)

In following through with that thought, John also reminds the church that there are only three things in the world that will destroy it, both individually and corporately: "the lust of the flesh, and the lust of the eyes, and the pride of life" (1 John 2:16). These, he says, are not of the Father, but of the world. The leaders of the church should remember that they are the same three things that brought sin into the world from the beginning as mentioned in Genesis 3:6. The Devil tried to trap Christ with the same method he used on Eve but was rebuked and defeated on all three points.

On the other hand, because of greed, status, fame, and popularity, many ministers have opened themselves up to the lure of fame over faith, cash over Christ, performance over anointing; acting over been lead by the Holy Spirit; self over service; greed over grace, and by all accounts have trivialized the ministry of the church into becoming nothing more than a place to bring your money and performance and be a social gathering. Jesus did turn over the tables of the moneychangers and rebuked them for turning his Father's house, which was designed to be a house of prayer, "into a den of thieves" (Luke 19:46).

One can't but wonder what must be going on in the mind of God as he watches the exploitation of his kingdom, designed to be a place of refuge and hope for the lost but has become a place for merchandising, fame, popularity, and celebrity status. Many who have started churches did not go into ministry because they were driven by the passion for the lost but because, by watching others, believed it was an opportunity for one to get rich quick.

There are many arguments out there for and against the concept of the seven churches being designed not just for their time but also as a representation of the whole life of the church as they fit into certain eras. While it is true, as some argue, that there is no specific

Scripture that addresses this issue, it cannot be ignored that there are significant comparisons reflected in the lives of these churches that fit the times mentioned.

As has been previously stated, none is more clear than the Laodecian church with its focus on gold, glamour, wealth, riches, pride, and fame but is found naked, (unclothed in righteousness), blind (still walking in the darkness of sin), rich (with earthly treasures) but poverty stricken, and functioning without the leading and influence of the Holy Spirit who alone gives life.

Whoever is a keen observer of the churches today will clearly see that there is a lot going on in terms of activities, programs, community outreach, and taking care of the needy, which is a godly thing to do. However, when lives are not being changed from within, the external things will have little importance as far as life (true life) in Christ is concerned. Activity should never take precedence over spirituality!

The mission of the church is to make disciples for Christ and preach the doctrine of the grace of God and redemption and reconciliation of the lost. But clearly, as seen, there is this gradual but constant drift from righteousness and a craving for things more than a desire Christ. By the grace and help of God, and by listening to the leading of the Spirit, the awareness of the danger of living carelessly in accordance with the world will be made clear and hopefully bring conviction that will cause people to come back to where Christ is the central focus of everyday living.

CHAPTER 1

THE SEVEN CHURCHES' GEOGRAPHICAL LOCATION

These churches will be discussed individually as they are unique in their strategic locations. It should be noted that they did not cover the greater portion of Asia Minor; rather, they were located to the far west. However, on a general basis, they were located near to the east of the Aegean Sea with Ephesus, Smyrna, and Pergamos much closer to the coastlines.

Asia Minor was located east of the Mediterranean Sea and south of the Black Sea within the Aegean section of the Mediterranean. This location is north and west of Babylon. It is present-day Turkey, which in biblical times was called Galatia and familiar with Paul's missionary journeys and writings.

Baker's Bible Atlas describes Asia Minor as "a peninsula in western Asia ... bounded on the north by the Black Sea, and on the south by the Mediterranean, and on the west by the Aegean arm of the Mediterranean. Today, it is part of the Turkish Republic known as Anatolia, which means 'the sunrise.'"[1] This is also north and west of the land of Israel. One can only imagine how Asia Minor has become a popular tourist attraction with millions of visitors annually, based on its rich history both in ancient times and its current status in the Middle East.

The apostle John who received the letters to the seven churches was exiled on the little island called Patmos, when and where he had his supernatural encounter with Christ and was given the crucial messages to the churches. The island was located southwest of Ephesus out in the Aegean waters. Patmos might not have been mentioned in biblical history had John not made his escape or been banished there. Today this small island is only about seven miles long by three miles wide according to some reports, though some of these reports are far apart on the statistics.

This little island at the end of the first century was not far away from many other small islands used by the Roman emperor to exile or banish political prisoners. For many centuries, this island was not inhabited and industrialized for fear of pirates, who regularly invade these small islands. But around 1088, a monk from Nicaea, Christodoulos Latrenus, was granted permission to build a monastery on the island. For many years, he made concerted efforts to memorialize some of the religious icons by building monasteries and chapels. These were built at strategic locations to honor the lives of prominent people. This made Christodoulos a well-known, revered, and honored man on Patmos to this day. It is said that the reverence and recognition he received is second only to the apostle John.

---

[1] White Wing Publishing House, *The Seven Churches of Asia*. "Know Your Bible Series" (Cleveland, Tenn.: White Wing Publishing House and Press, 2002), 5.

Christodoulos receives continued recognition by the people who inhabit the island of Patmos, for each year he is honored twice on the island. One of the times he is honored is the memorial of his death and the other is the time his remains were brought to Patmos from a neighboring island, where he actually died.

What was once an isolated, lonely island has now become a visitor's dream. As one author puts it,

> Famous for being the location for the writing of the book of Revelation (the Apocalypse), the island of Patmos is a jewel in the Aegean. This small island combines the charm and beauty of a typical Greek island with the tranquility and reverence of a sacred space. Visitors today might very well wish that they, like John, could be sentenced to exile on this island so rich with tradition, faith, and wonder.[2]

It is important to note the order in which the churches were addressed. These churches may have been strategically positioned by location and character, especially if it is to be believed that they represent specific eras in the ecclesiastical church history. There is no doubt that God in his infinite wisdom and omniscience had it all figured out, especially since he intended to use these churches as examples to Christendom on a general level.

Clearly, throughout history God used people, scenarios, circumstances, symbolism, types, and shadows to create awareness for all generations. So taking a look at Patmos and where it was located, immediately southwest of Ephesus, Ephesus was the closest in proximity for the first letter as John made his exit from Patmos. Noting how God has worked through history gives the assurance

---

2   Clyde E. Fant and Mitchell G. Reddish, *A Guide to Biblical Sites in Greece and Turkey* (New York: Oxford University Press, 2003, 92.

that nothing done by God is by chance or happenstance. God has all things figured out, and the things that are mysterious to the human mind is just another day at the office (using an old cliché) for the Lord.

John made his exodus from Patmos to Ephesus going northeast. These churches were positioned in a horseshoe or triangular form not far from one another, so when John left Ephesus, he continued further north to Smyrna and then to Pergamos, which is the farthest north of the seven churches.

Leaving Pergamos, he went southeast to Thyatira, continued south to Sardis and Philadelphia, and finally to Laodicea. This whole area is rich in biblical history, even going further east into Lystra, Derbe, Tarsus—the hometown of Saul or Tarsus, who became the renowned apostle Paul—and continuing farther east and south into Antioch to Lebanon, Damascus, Sidon, Tyre, and Jerusalem.

This gives a clear geographical picture of how John left Patmos and journeyed to these churches one by one. He didn't have electronic devices and social media to get his message out. Chances are, he walked to each of these churches, or at best was obliged by riding an ass or a mule. It proves, however, how amazing God is in how he affords the church the ability throughout the many eras to accomplish its duties and ministries using the available resources to its advantage.

A Lot in Common

All these churches had something in common: they were encouraged to listen to what the Spirit was saying to reap the benefits provided. Five out of the seven churches were not operating at the level Christ expected while two were encouraged for having suffered and persevered through very hard times. The other five were rebuked and admonished to make changes or face the consequences of not listening to the voice of the Spirit. While there are apostles, prophets, pastors, preachers, teachers, and evangelists, the Spirit of God through his Word must be the dominant voice listened to above all. This also shows that a church cannot effectively operate when the Spirit is not heard or listened to.

The letters Jesus gave John all had a certain pattern to them. They were addressed to the angels of the churches and sent directly to the shepherd or overseer, who had the responsibility to ensure that the church as a body was informed about Christ's findings and admonitions and what steps would be required to make corrections.

The angel of the church was who God held accountable for taking or not taking the steps to instruct the church and lead them by example into making the necessary changes. The interpretations of who the angels were differ among commentators, but regardless of who one concludes the angels might have been, the messages are unchanged.

Another thing these churches had in common was the promise that if they did as they were instructed, they would be rewarded. God is a God of promises, and he will fulfill his promises because he is the almighty God, he needs no counsel, he is self-existent, and he makes decisions all by himself. But the responsibility is always on the people who are instructed to do as God requires of them in order to reap the benefits of his blessings.

Following God's instructions historically has provided tremendous benefits to his people. These letters bring to light Paul's letter to Timothy concerning the application of God's Word to his life. In the same manner, all who apply God's Word to their daily lives will reap the benefits to be derived.

> All Scripture is given by inspiration of God, and is profitable for doctrine, (to teach one the fundamentals of the Christian faith, and how he should live) for reproof, (to provide the evidence or proof of our wrongs, and bring conviction); for correction, (to tell us how to make our wrongs right, how to fall back in line with God); for instruction in righteousness, (to let the people know how to avoid falling back into the same predicament: in other words, for chastening and

guidance into walking in justification); That the man of God may perfect, (complete, fully mature); thoroughly furnished (well equipped with all the tools necessary) unto all good works. (2 Timothy 3:16–17, emphasis added)

Here is something of great interest and worthy of observation: As Jesus sent the letters to all of the churches, he identified himself in seven different ways to each of them. A broader look will be taken when observing the different descriptions in looking at the churches individually, but here is a preview of how he introduced himself to the seven churches. First, Ephesus: "These things saith he that holdeth the seven stars in his right hand, who walketh in the midst of the seven golden candlesticks." Second, Smyrna: "These things saith the first and the last, which was dead, and is alive." Third, Pergamos: "These things saith he which hath the sharp sword with two edges." Fourth, Thyatira: "These things saith the Son of God, who hath his eyes like unto a flame of fire, and his feet are like fine brass." Fifth, Sardis: "These things saith he that hath the seven Spirits of God, and the seven stars." Sixth, Philadelphia: "These things saith he that is holy, he that is true, he that hath the key of David, he that openeth, and no man shutteth, and he that shutteth and no man openeth." Seventh, Laodicea: "These things saith the Amen, the faithful and true witness, the beginning of the creation of God."

This should be an interesting study of what all these different descriptions meant to the churches individually. The theme that followed consistently, no matter how he introduced himself, was his omniscience. "I know thy works!" They all had been through different experiences and had their own personalities, actions, and reactions, but when it was all over, they were admonished in a similar manner: "He that hath an ear, let him hear what the Spirit saith unto the churches"(Revelation 2:7). This statement cannot be ignored at any point in the life of the church.

One can only make wrongs right or build his hope and confidence by listening to the wooing of the Spirit. He is the one who searches the heart, reveals the world of sin and judgment, and instructs in the path of righteousness.

Everyone individually or all collectively should learn from this instruction and never fall into the predicament these churches found themselves in. There are always voices vying for the attention of the church. The Devil is like a roaring lion, seeking whom he may devour, but likewise is the Spirit of God speaking constantly, creating an awareness of the craftiness of the Devil. So a listening ear must constantly be given to the voice of the Holy Spirit when he speaks. He does not always speak with a loud voice (as the Devil does, trying to convince men to listen), but often he reasons deep within the inner man with a still, small voice.

CHAPTER 2

THE REVELATION OF JESUS CHRIST

The book of Revelation appropriately begins with "The revelation of Jesus Christ" because there are many things that would be revealed throughout the chapters. Beginning by looking at the word revelation, the Greek word is *apokalupsis* (apocalypse), which speaks of revealing or unveiling that which God chooses to do throughout dispensations as he sees fit or necessary.

In the book of Revelation are many things yet to be fulfilled that have been revealed to John, which creates an awareness and gives a better understanding of things to come and how they will finally fall into place. So the revelation is to remove the veil to uncover the things that were locked up for millennia.

One example of the things unveiled in the book is Daniel's vision when he was told by the angel Gabriel, "But thou, O Daniel, shut up the words, and seal the book, even to the time of the end" (Daniel 12:4). This vision was sealed until Christ the Holy One came and opened the book, as John stated, "And I wept much, because no man was found worthy to open and to read the book, neither to look thereon," but as he mourned and contemplated, he was told by one of the elders, "Weep not: behold, the Lion of the tribe of Judah, the Root of David, hath prevailed to open the book, and to loose the seven seals thereof" (Revelation 5:4–5).

The complicated things that perplexed Daniel, causing Gabriel's release from heaven to give him clarity, have been made clearer to John in the Revelation of Jesus Christ. "It is not so much a revelation or unveiling of the Person of Christ, though it discloses His High Priestly and Kingly glory, as it is, however, the unveiling of those events that shall precede and accompany His return to the earth."[3]

According to what John was told, these things would shortly come to pass. These things were pointed out or announced by the angel, making the record clear. That these things will take place shortly or swiftly may be interpreted in many ways by different people, but as it can be recalled, God's timing does not fit with man's timeline. The ancient Greek word for "shortly," *en,* is a primitive preposition denoting something that is fixed or in place. It also suggests that the time is set and will not be changed. It could be misunderstood for "coming soon," which is not what this is implying, but rather, whenever it happens, it will happen quickly, unexpectedly, and constantly. David Guzik says, "Quickly or suddenly coming to pass, indicating rapidity or execution after the beginning takes place. The idea is not that the event may occur soon, but rather when it does, it will be sudden."[4]

---

[3] Clarence Larkin, *The Book of Revelation:* (Rev. Clarence Larkin Estate, 1919), 1.

[4] David Guzik, *"Study Guide for Revelation 2."* Enduring Word. Blue Letter Bible. 7 Jul 2006. http://www.blueletterbible.org/Comm/guzik_david/StudyGuide_Rev/Rev_2.cfm. (accessed February 12, 2013).

The Importance of the Book

How important is this book? To some, it's scary, hard to understand, and difficult to explain. Because of that, many preachers do not even touch it. But if preachers do not understand, preach, and teach this book, there will be a lot missing in what the church should expect in the times of the end and also at the end of times. "Blessed is he that readeth, and they that hear the words of this prophecy, and keep those things which are written therein: for the time is at hand" (Revelation 1:4).

There is something unique and special about this book if one reads and understands its contents and context. It is not inconceivable to wonder if it's because of the blessings attached to it why the Devil makes so many people stay away from it. The Greek word *makareos* for "blessed" speaks of a prolonged form of blessing (supremely blessed). By extension, it refers to being fortunate or well off. That is a great thought!

This should be an encouragement and a driving force for preachers with an anticipated gratification to want to dig deeper into this treasure and reap the benefits God offers to those who read, hear, and keep the sayings of this great book. This cannot be overlooked. "The book of Revelation gives us much more than information for prophetic speculation. It gives us things to keep. If we understand the book of Revelation, it will change the way we live."[5]

God is amazing in this expression. He caters not only to the educated or literate but also to the uneducated and illiterate; not only to those with the ability to read will reap the benefits but also those who listen to the reading and follow its directives. The blessing is not limited to certain people. Do you ever wonder why this book is so

---

5   David Guzik, *"Study Guide for Revelation 2."* Enduring Word. Blue Letter Bible. 7 Jul 2006. http://www.blueletterbible.org/Comm/guzik_david/StudyGuide_Rev/Rev_2.cfm. (accessed February 12, 2013).

feared or ignored? The great rebuke of the churches, the identifying of the last days apostate church, the admonition to the believers to buy Christ's gold that is tried in fire so they can be rich and clothed in white raiment is what the Devil wants to disguise. How about his facing his own fate? Chances are, the Devil wants to prevent the readers from understanding what God has in store for him.

The book of Revelation clearly describes the fate of the Devil, and no doubt he hates for the believer to fully understand his eternal destiny. Here, John brings a sevenfold salutation to the churches and, at the same time, exalts Christ and reminds the church of his sure return. The message to the churches started in chapter 1 with the exaltation of Christ and warning of his return. "Grace be unto you, and peace, from him which is, and was, and which is to come; and from the seven Spirits which are before his throne" (Revelation 1:4).

The Seven Spirits

Just looking at the expression "seven spirits" and putting into perspective the message that was conveyed to the churches is mind-boggling. Why seven spirits? Is there more than one Spirit? Of course not. It is well known that there is but one Spirit of God. It is also known that he is called and referenced by many names and titles, but here it takes another twist for the human mind. The seven mentioned here is believed by many commentators and theologians not to refer to numbers because the Holy Spirit is one. However, the number seven speaks of his completeness and perfection. David Guzik again puts it into perspective.

> The idea of the seven Spirits quote from the Old Testament (Isaiah 11:2) describes seven aspects of the Holy Spirit: The Spirit of the Lord shall rest upon him, the Spirit of wisdom and understanding, the Spirit of counsel and might, the

> Spirit of knowledge and fear of the Lord. It isn't that there are seven different spirits of God, rather the Spirit of the Lord has these characteristics, and He has them all in fullness and perfection.[6]

This is great when one thinks of the fullness of the Holy Spirit that Isaiah described. Though Jesus is Father, Son, and Holy Spirit in one, the complete function of the Spirit is leading one in doing the will of God. Jesus himself made reference to the power of the Holy Spirit upon him as he read from the same prophet, Isaiah.

> The Spirit of the Lord is upon me, because he hath anointed me to preach the gospel to the poor; he hath sent me to heal the broken hearted, to preach deliverance to the captives, and recovering of sight to the blind, to set at liberty them that are bruised, to preach the acceptable year of the Lord. (Luke 4:18)

This sevenfold salutation that came from Jesus Christ, the faithful witness and first begotten of the dead, has a couple important things to note in this statement. One, Christ is described as the "faithful witness." This is important because he is laying the groundwork for when he begins to address the churches individually. It is like in a courthouse trial there are witnesses who the lawyers and jurors consider credible. It is established here that Jesus is, and will be, a credible witness. He told Nicodemus, "We speak that we do know, and testify that we have seen; and ye receive not our witness" (John 3:11). So his character and credibility is not in question.

---

6   David Guzik, *"Study Guide for Revelation 2."* Enduring Word. Blue Letter Bible. 7 Jul 2006. http://www.blueletterbible.org/Comm/guzik_david/StudyGuide_Rev/Rev_2.cfm. (accessed February 12, 2013).

Two, he's the first begotten of the dead. "First begotten" does not give him a birthdate or suggest there are more after him, though it is known that his mother, Mary, had more children. But Jesus was the only begotten Son of God. It is not implying that he was created, as some suggest, because in Hebrews 2:7 it reads, "Thou madest him a little lower than the angels; thou crownedst him with glory and honor, and didst set him over the works of thy hands" (also mentioned in Psalm 8:5). This sets him apart from all, not only because he is the "first fruit of them that slept" but also because he has preeminence over the living and the dead, now and in the future, all through the resurrections of both the saints and sinners. Clarence Larkin has this to say about him as the faithful witness: "He is called the 'Faithful Witness,' as such he is a PROPHET. As the 'First Begotten From The Dead,' He carried His own blood into the Heavenly Tabernacle, and thus performed the work of a PRIEST."[7]

Jesus performing the office of a priest was like no other priests, who were a type of Christ, who often offered the blood of animals. But as the writer of Hebrews states, "Neither by the blood of goats and calves, but by his own blood he entered in once into the holy place, having obtained eternal redemption for us" (Hebrews 9:12). This, of course, made him the great or greatest high priest, who "through his own blood" expiates the sins from the sinner and leaves him justified. All other priests offered the blood of animals, but Christ offered his own.

John continued the theme of the book that speaks constantly about Christ's return. He made it clear that Christ is coming in the clouds, and all eyes shall see him. How can one forget the eternal existence of Christ who is from everlasting to everlasting? Just in case one would forget, the message was reiterated, "I am Alpha and Omega,

---

7   Clarence Larkin, *The Book of Revelation:* (Rev. Clarence Larkin Estate, 1919), 6.

the beginning and the ending, which is, which was, and which is to come, the Almighty" (Revelation 1:8).

John was on the isle called Patmos after escaping death when he had this experience with the Lord Jesus Christ. Being in the Spirit on the Lord's Day, this experience was completely dominated by the Spirit's presence and power. Saturated with the divine influence, John lost contact with the outside world and was devoid of external distractions. His life was completely revolutionized. At this crucial juncture in his life, having being on the isle of Patmos for approximately thirteen years, he heard the voice of Christ like a trumpet, reminding him of the eternal existence of Christ and instructing him that the things he was about to see he should write in a book and send to the seven churches.

An added thought as to why John was told to write could be pointed back to the prophets in the Old Testament. Many things God showed and told the prophets, they did not write, but there are some things God told them to write because it should be on the record for preservation. It would not be too far-fetched to imagine that, had God not told John to write, he may have taken it for granted and missed the moment. So God did not trust his judgment and told him to write it down and take it to the churches. It should be noted that there were more than seven churches in the vicinity, but special attention was given to these.

As said above, this is the Revelation of Jesus Christ, not only in words but also in credible form depicted or illustrated by John in Revelation 1:12–16. Anyone who had John's experience would have had the same reaction he did. "And when I saw him" (as he tries to give a glimpse of the profound effect it had on him), "I fell at his feet as dead." This experience was like none he'd ever had, and remember, he was one of Jesus' closest friends. But none of his past experiences with Christ prepared him for this moment. "And he laid his right hand upon me, saying unto me, Fear not; I am the first and the last: I am he that liveth and was dead; and, behold I am alive for evermore, and have the keys of hell and death" (Revelation 1:17–18). Having the keys of both hell and death, suggests a couple of things. First, "the keys" imply absolute power and authority, and second, "hell" *(hah'-dace or Hades)*, the place or state of the departed souls, also speaks of the grave. Third, "death" *(than'-at-os)* is a word used as an adjective or as a noun and speaks of death literally or figuratively. If he has the keys of hell and death, he has absolute power and authority and demands respect and reverence. As George Grace said,

> With regard to the "keys of hell and of death," Revelation 3:7 notes that Christ is "he that hath the key of David, he that openeth, and no man shutteth; and shutteth, and no man openeth." This includes the "key to the bottomless pit" from which the Antichrist will come in the Tribulation. (Revelation 9:1–11; 11:17)[8]

There is something powerful about having the key. It gives you access to everything that key opens and allows you to lock anything that the key fits. The message was clear: all the churches understood the basic premise of one having the key. Doctor Peter Ruckman makes mention of a number of keys and what they symbolize.

> The Bible speaks of a number of keys. We find the "key of David" that is called promises. We have the "key of knowledge" that is called law. We have the "key of the kingdom" that is called gospel. We have the "key of the bottomless pit" that is called judgment. Here our Lord has the keys of death and

---

8   George Grace, *The Study of Revelation*: (First Bible Baptist Church, Rochester, NY 2010), 26.

hell. Thank God for that! My Savior has the keys, and more than that, He is the door. (John 10:9)[9]

Here, John is instructed to write the things that he has seen; the "things which are," the current status of the churches as given to him in chapters 2–3, the "things which shall be hereafter," which refers to the churches as they are recorded in Revelation 4 and throughout the entire book.

The Seven Stars

Now it's time to look at the mystery of the seven stars, and it is indeed a mystery.

There are many different schools of thought concerning who or what these seven stars were that John saw in Jesus' right hand. There is a greater consensus concerning the lampstands because Jesus made it clear that "and the seven lampstands that thou sawest are the seven churches." Without controversy, the lampstands are the churches themselves, but the seven stars that are mentioned are the angels of the seven churches. For some, they are much more complicated. However, it will be easier to agree with the view of the stars being the pastors of the churches.

A quick look at a number of the views will give you a chance to draw a conclusion in determining who these really are. The Greek word used here for "angels" is *angelos* or messengers of the churches. Some commentators believe these angels are heavenly representatives, which is hard to justify because heavenly beings are unlikely to be the messengers of local churches. It would also be unlikely for Christ to

---

9   Peter S. Ruckman, *The Book of Revelation:* (BB Bookstore, Pensacola, FL 1970), Loc. 681.

give John messages to take to heavenly beings, as they would be in heaven with Christ. But as promised, you can take a look at some of the arguments, and then it will be easier to decide.

Among the different arguments presented, Clarence Larkin says, "We are told in verse 20 that the 'Seven Stars' stand for the 'ANGELS' of the 'Seven Churches.' These 'Angels' are not angelic beings but Messengers of the churches."[10] This is likely to be the most reasonable thought when compared with many others, for not all have this conviction. He continues to say,

> What a beautiful and solemn lesson is taught here. It is that the ministers of Christ derive power and office from Him, and that He holds them in His hand. If they are false to Him, no one can deliver them from His power, and if they are true and loyal, no one can touch or molest, or do them harm.[11]

There is another argument by Peter Ruckman, which is on the other side of the coin, as he believes both the stars and "angels" are representatives in heaven and, going even a bit further, puts the candlestick in heaven too. This is his view on the interpretation. Looking at the seven stars, which are the angels of the seven churches, he said, "Then each of these churches has an angelic representative in heaven called 'a star' ... then each church has a candlestick in heaven represented by candlestick burning, with a flame on it."[12]

This for some is a bit off the charts, but it is for you to contemplate and conclude. There is another set of arguments in which one can judge, for example, as David Guzik says, "Some people believe that the angels are the pastors of these seven churches. This idea is based

---

10 Clarence Larkin, The Book of Revelation: (Rev. Clarence Larkin Estate, 1919), 12.
11 Ibid 12.
12 Peter S.Ruckman, The Book of Revelation: (BB Bookstore, Pensacola, FL 1970), Loc. 695.

on a literal understanding of the ancient Greek word translated angel, *angelos*. That word literally means 'messenger,' and certainly pastors are 'messengers' to the churches."[13]

Although he also made the point that others believe these are guardian angels over each congregation, he quotes Adam Clarke, who believes the pastors are the actual angels John was sent to. David Guzik writes, "Adam Clarke believed the angel of each church was the pastor. 'Angel of the church here answers exactly to that office of the synagogue among the Jews called ... messenger of the church, whose business it was to read, pray, and teach in the synagogue."[14]

As one commentator says, there are strengths and weaknesses in both arguments, but the strongest of them must be that the angel of the church is the pastor, which appears to be the most rational for the reason that has been given previously. It is virtually clear where some have missed this by comparing the concept of individuals having guardian angels to churches having the same. However, it must be reiterated that there is little to no logic in having Christ tell John to take messages to angels when angels are heavenly beings.

So here is the conclusion with a little nugget from Jamieson, Fausset & Brown's commentary on the topic:

> For how could heavenly angels be charged with the delinquencies laid here to the charge of these angels? Then, if a human angel be meant (as the Old Testament analogy favors Hag. 1:13, "the Lord's Messenger in the Lord's message"

---

13 David Guzik, *"Study Guide for Revelation 2."* Enduring Word. Blue Letter Bible. 7 Jul 2006. http://www.blueletterbible.org/Comm/guzik_david/StudyGuide_Rev/Rev_2.cfm (accessed February 12, 2013).

14 Ibid.

Mal. 2:7; 3:1), the bishop, or superintendent pastor, must be the angel.[15]

The fact that these churches needed to take action from the rebuke and admonition they received concludes, without a doubt, that the angels of each church is the head leader, which comes down to the shepherd/pastor.

---

15   Jamieson, Robert; A.R. Fausset; and David Brown. "Commentary on Revelation 2." .Blue Letter Bible. 19 Feb 2000. http://www.blueletterbible.org/Comm/jfb/Rev/Rev_002.cfm (accessed September 13, 2013).

CHAPTER 3

EPHESUS

Ephesus is a well-known place in Asia Minor that had a long history, both positive and negative. There will be a lot discovered about this small province strategically located near the coastline of the Aegean Sea, not very far east of Greece.

Ephesus dates back to 1044 BC and has seen more than its fair share of controlling powers that dominates its history. There was a group of Ionian Greek settlers who made their dwelling there in the early days of its beginnings.

> Ephesus is situated near the Aegean coast, east and slightly north of the island of Samos and approximately 40 miles south of Izmir ... In antiquity Ephesus was a major port city situated on the Aegean coast. Over the years alluvial deposits from the Cayster River, which ran near the city, filled in the harbor, an as a result, the site of the city today

lies approximately 5 miles inland from the coast. Over the years alluvial deposits from the Cayster River, which ran near the city, filled in the harbor, and as a result, the site of the city today lies approximately 5 miles inland from the coast. In addition, Ephesus was the beginning point for main highway that ran from the Aegean coast to the eastern part of Anatolia which along with its harbor allowed the city to flourish as a commercial and transportation center.[16]

Ephesus had an ancient history as a major highway, making it possible for trading and transporting commercial goods back and forth to Anatolia. This built the city's status as a commercial destination, which caused the city to flourish. Ephesus was known for its well-established religious practices and was also considered as one of the great cities of ancient times. It was so popular, especially with great roads and commercial activities, that it once gained the name "Vanity Fair of Asia."

Eventually, Ephesus did not have the fortitude to withstand the challenges it would face over the many years. Croesus of Lydia conquered Ephesus around 560 BCE.

> A member of the **Mermnad dynasty**, Croesus succeeded to the throne of his father, Alyattes, after a struggle with his half-brother. Croesus is said to have acted as viceroy and commander in chief before his father's death. He completed his conquest of mainland Ionia by capturing Ephesus and other cities in western Anatolia.[17]

---

16 Clyde E. Fant and Mitchell G. Reddish, A Guide to Biblical Sites in Greece and Turkey: (New York: Oxford University Press, 2003), 177.

17 Encyclopedia Britannica, http://www.britannica.com/EBchecked/topic/143732/Croesus (accessed September 12, 2013).

As a result of this conquest, there was great decline in the life and power of the city as Croesus moved it farther south. Croesus faced his own demise when Cyrus of Persia defeated him and Ephesus came under Persian control. It was during this time that the temple of Artemis was built for the worship of Artemis (the goddess, Diana) and was revered for its religious symbolism.

> Disaster struck the city in 356 BCE, when fire destroyed the Artemision. Alexander the Great, who was reportedly born on the same day as the Artemision fire, took over the area in 334 BCE. His offer to finance the ongoing reconstruction of the temple was diplomatically declined by the Ephesians, who said that it was not fitting for one god to make a dedication for another God.[18]

Eventually, the temple was rebuilt with unimaginable architecture and splendor, so it became one of the Seven Wonders of the Ancient World.

On the side of general Christianity, Ephesus had its fair share of Christians, and some of the greatest counsel and instruction was found in the New Testament. There was no prominence of Jewish synagogues in ancient Ephesus, though some believed there was at least a remnant of Jews there.

> No remains of a synagogue or Jewish artifacts have been found in ancient Ephesus. Likewise, few Jewish inscriptions have been found. Several literary works, however, attest to the presence of Jews in the city. The 1st-century Jewish historian Josephus on several occasions mentions Jews in Ephesus, pointing our certain privileges they enjoyed (such

---

18 Clyde E. Fant and Mitchell G. Reddish, A Guide to Biblical Sites in Greece and Turkey: (New York: Oxford University Press, 2003), 178.

as exemption from Roman military service and the freedom to practice their religion). The book of Acts (see below) also describes a Jewish community in Ephesus, including a Jewish synagogue. Christianity arrived early in Ephesus, apparently introduced by Paul, Priscilla, and Aquila (Acts 18:18-19). The book of revelation gives evidence of Christians in the city at the end of the 1st century CE. (2:1-7)[19]

The apostle Paul spent about three years ministering in this city as recorded in Acts: "Therefore watch, (he said) and remember, that by the space of three years I ceased not to warn every one night and day with tears" (Acts 20:31). It appears that Paul through the Spirit foresaw what was coming up against this church—he warned and encouraged them, but they did not maintain their Christian standard. It would be of great benefit if you read Acts 20 beginning at verse 17 to see how Paul called the elders together and had them listen to him as he poured out his heart for the life, faith, and victory of the church. But as Job said, "For the thing which I greatly feared is come upon me, and that which I was afraid of is come into me" (Job 3:25).

So it was, as Paul made his fears clear, there was still the decline and backsliding of the church. Although they tried to identify and resist false teachers and false apostles, their endurance did not last, and they fell away from their first love. Prior to looking at the first letter to the Ephesians, it is pertinent to take a glimpse at the epistle of Paul the apostle to the Ephesians.

Finis Jennings Dake, in his summary of Ephesians, considers it to be the second doctrinal letter, and that it pictures the believer sitting with Christ in heavenly places. He believes it contains the highest of church truth but not church order and is second only to the Romans

---

19 Clyde E. Fant and Mitchell G. Reddish, A Guide to Biblical Sites in Greece and Turkey: (New York: Oxford University Press, 2003), 180.

letter that sets forth the true relation of the believer to Christ in death, burial, and resurrection. There are some who believe that this epistle was not necessarily written exclusively to the Ephesians but to the broader Christian community. It has some of the richest thoughts and is loaded with instructions concerning a believer's position in Christ through grace. It covers the church, addresses how a Christian should live, gives believers a look into the mystery of Christ and his church, and admonishes the church to be prepared for spiritual warfare, using the example of the natural armor to protect oneself against the wiles and fiery darts of the Wicked One.

This epistle was written when Paul was in prison in Rome (around AD 61–64), where he encouraged the church through his letters. None of his epistles covered more topics than this one. If the epistle to the Ephesians is studied and understood, it would not be hard to consider it as a favorite because of the richness of its content. With this in mind, it would be an injustice not to pause and take a brief look at some of the great thoughts and admonitions laid out in these six incredible chapters.

Ephesus is the alpha (first of the seven churches), and the Laodicean church will be the omega (last of the seven churches). These two churches will take precedence in attention. So before taking a look at the church in Ephesus, a little time will be spent setting the stage for what lead to the letter to the church at Ephesus.

One writer calls the letter to the Ephesians the "Rolls Royce of the epistles." One can see through this epistle why the church of Ephesus was considered to have "left its first love." Bob Deffingbaugh, in his article "The Uniqueness of Ephesians Among the Epistles," writes,

> Apart from the Epistle to the Romans, few who have studied Paul's Epistles would challenge the statement that it is the "Rolls Royce of the epistles." F.F. Bruce, noted New Testament scholar, calls Ephesians "the quietness of Paulinism," C.H. Dodd called Ephesians "the crown of

Paulinism." According to William Hendrickson, Ephesians has been called "the divinest composition of man, the distilled essence of the Christian religion, the most authoritative and most consummate compendium of the Christian faith, full to the brim with thoughts and doctrines sublime and momentous."[20]

It is hard to resist this thought because it speaks the language of the heart. If you have never examined this epistle, now would be an ideal time to take the challenge. One of the unique things about it is that it's not dealing with a particular issue at a given church. It was not written to specific people like Timothy, Titus, or Philemon, or addressing known problems that was affecting the church at the time. The Galatians had problems with the law that Paul had to address, reminding them that their salvation was complete in Christ without circumcision.

"Ephesians is not a didactic (teaching) epistle. The Epistle to the Ephesians is written to one of the most well-taught churches that ever existed. Paul spent nearly 3 years teaching in Ephesus. Apollos had ministered there as well. And in Paul's absence he wrote two epistles to this group of believers."[21]

Taking a brief look at some of the great thoughts in the chapters will give a synopsis of the whole epistle and bring more light to the backslidden church of Ephesus.

Chapter 1:4ff makes clear that God had chosen the people before the foundation of the world, and made known the mystery of his will. After they believed, they were sealed with the Holy Spirit of promise.

---

20 Bob Deffingbaugh, https://bible.org/seriespage/1-uniqueness-ephesians-among-epistles 1. (accessed August 28, 2013).
21 Bob Deffingbaugh, https://bible.org/seriespage/1-uniqueness-ephesians-among-epistles 8. (accessed August 28, 2013).

In chapter 2, they were reminded that God had quickened (brought to life) all of them who were dead in trespasses and sins, where in time past they walked according to the course of this world (verses 1–3).

This is important because later we will see that there was a massive diversion from this admonition in the letter Jesus sent to them. They were reminded (in verses 8–9) that they were saved by grace through faith, and not of works.

In the conversation as it pertains to adoption, the Gentiles had a new position in Christ, made possible by the blood of Christ.

> For he is our peace, who hath made both one, and hath broken down the middle wall of partition between us; having abolished in his flesh the enmity, even the law of commandments contained in ordinances ... that he might reconcile both unto God in one body by the cross, having slain the enmity thereby. (Ephesians 2:14–16)

In 3:5–6, things that were not made known to the sons of men were now revealed unto God's holy apostles and prophets. "How that the Gentiles should be fellowheirs, and of the same body, and partakers of his promise in Christ by the gospel." How about Paul's beseeching them, having written this epistle from behind the prison walls in Rome as the prisoner of the Lord, that they walk worthy of the vocation to which they were called? They were encouraged to persevere, be tolerant, and bear with one another for the purpose of keeping the unity of the Spirit in the bond of peace.

He discussed what is called the fivefold ministry, which is actually fourfold. Of course, this is the portion of Scripture of which so many today are enamored. They develop their own concept and execution of those ministries designed for the perfection of the saints and edification of the body of Christ.

In 4:23ff, they are instructed what to put off, what to put on, and what to put away. Just reading these powerful statements from the apostle Paul stirs the emotions if one puts himself in the position of the Ephesians with the teacher and counselor giving what seems to be his last words to the church. He was encouraging them not to grieve the Holy Spirit wherewith they were sealed unto the day of redemption. All bitterness, wrath, malice, clamor, and evil speaking (past and future) should be put away.

What happened to the seven churches in Asia Minor, and especially the church at Ephesus, is not exclusive to this church. Taking a look at churches today, the same can be seen occurring. Anyone who does not take heed to what he has been taught and instructed by God's Word, will find himself in the same predicament of backsliding and walking away from his first love. In a world where anything goes, and unfortunately as seen in some churches, the apostle in 5:3–5 points out some specific things that are even more detrimental to the Christian walk: "But fornication and all uncleanness, or covetousness, let it not be once named among you, as becometh saints; neither filthiness, nor foolish talking, nor jesting, which are not convenient: but rather giving of thanks."

Everywhere today are numerous teachings and teachers. There are more apostles and prophets than there were in the apostle's time, and this is not due to the vast difference in population. With the rapid speed of prophetic and apostolic growth, it is clear that these teachings have become more important to the church. Again, God clearly foresaw the times the church would be experiencing and warned them to be aware.

While Christ's warning in Matthew 24 speaks predominantly of end times and his second coming, it cannot be overlooked that the church is on the threshold of this time, so it behooves God's church to be on the alert. One wonders, Why is there a school of prophets? Why is there a "school for apostolic development"? These seem to be leading up to the fulfillment of the words of Christ: "For there shall arise false Christs, and false prophets, and shall shew great signs and wonders; insomuch that, if it were possible, they shall deceive the very elect" (Matthew 24:24). Although Matthew is pointing out things that will happen during the great tribulation, these were the very heretic challenges the churches were facing, which is why they were admonished to be on the watch for deceivers.

Today, everywhere there is someone with a word of prophecy to be delivered specifically to a person or family. There is a miracle that God wants to do, but it often comes with a price tag. This will be dealt with in greater detail when we look at the Laodicean church. But these are the things that caused the apostle Paul great concern and why he told the Ephesians, "Let no man deceive you with vain words: for because of these things cometh the wrath of God upon the children of disobedience" (Ephesians 5:6).

The apostle Paul gave them counsel on their domestic lives, although this is one of the most used, and sometimes misunderstood, portion of Scripture regarding how the wife and husband should love, respect, and honor each other. It teaches that there should be mutual submission to one another, and that husbands should love their wives like Christ loves the church and gave himself for it.

Finally, in chapter 6, children are encouraged to obey and honor their parents, fathers are to avoid provoking their children to wrath, servants are to obey their masters, masters are to treat their servants with dignity, and, in the conclusion, they are instructed how to protect themselves from the wiles of the Devil. He used a military term, *armor*, to indicate the level of spiritual preparation the church will need to protect itself against the onslaught of the Enemy.

The church is instructed to wear full armor, both defensive and offensive, and the appropriate weapons necessary to fight and defend against the fiery darts of the Wicked One. In Acts 20, when Paul was sent to Ephesus to the elders of the church, he reminded them of his coming to Asia and that he kept back nothing that was profitable unto them. At this sad moment, however, he told them they would see him no more, and that he would not be responsible for what happened after he left: "Wherefore I take you to record this day, that I am pure from the blood of all men. For I have not shunned to declare unto you all the counsel of God" (vv. 26–27).

One of the more interesting things in this conversation is that Paul told the elders to take heed unto themselves and the flock over which they had been made overseers to feed the church of God, which he had purchased with his own blood. What is even more intriguing is that he foresaw the danger the church would face and did everything to prepare them. Again, no doubt God was preparing the church for the things that were to come. He saw men like grievous wolves coming in, not sparing the flock.

They were also admonished to prepare themselves for criticism and slander. "For I know this, that after my departing shall grievous wolves enter in among you, not sparing the flock. Also your own selves shall men arise, speaking perverse things, to draw away disciples after them" (vv. 29–30). When one reads and assesses these verses, the heart breaks when seeing what happened even after such great counsel and instruction to preempt the imminent attack of the Enemy. If they had on the whole armor of God as recorded in chapter 6, they would have been protected from all that was thrown at them.

But that did not happen, and unfortunately, the church went into apostasy, which warrants Christ's letter to the first of the churches, Ephesus. "But he that knew not, and did commit things worthy of stripes, shall be beaten with few *stripes*. For unto whomsoever much is given, of him shall be much required: and to whom men have committed much, of him they will ask the more" (Luke 12:48, emphasis added). Unfortunately, so much was invested in this church, but it still fell from its first love.

CHAPTER 4

THE CHURCH OF EPHESUS

The church of Ephesus was located on the western coast of Asia Minor near the Aegean Sea. It was approximately forty miles south of Izmir and was situated south of Smyrna and Pergamos and northeast of Patmos. This was an interesting province with a strong religious background. The worship of Artemis (the Greek goddess of the moon) was prevalent. "The Roman name for Artemis was Diana. The Temple of Diana was one of the ancient 'Seven Wonders of the World.'"[22]

When Paul went to Ephesus, he faced challenges and opposition from the worshippers of Diana. However, when he got there, he found disciples of John who were baptized in water but were not taught

---

22 White Wing Publishing House, *The Seven Churches of Asia*. "Know your Bible Series" (White Wing Publishing House and Press, Cleveland, Tennessee, 2002), 20.

about the baptism of the Holy Ghost, as recorded in Acts 19. "He said unto them, have ye received the Holy Ghost since ye believed ... we have not so much as heard of whether there be any Holy Ghost" (v. 2). He continued to ask them unto what then were they baptized, and when they told him, "unto John's baptism," Paul counseled them and baptized them again in water. Dake in his commentary on Acts 19:5 puts it well when he says,

> They were baptized over in water, so they could conform to Christian water baptism "in the name of the Father, and of the Son, and of the Holy Ghost" (Mt. 28:19). They never had been baptized this way. They only knew the name of God, for John did not know the Son until a certain sign happened (Jn. 1:33). So he could not have baptized except in the name of God (John 5:43).[23]

This is an interesting thought for those who take out of context the statement by Luke that they were "baptized in the name of the Lord Jesus." They justify baptizing in "Jesus' name" and not "Father, Son, and Holy Ghost," using this passage and also Acts 2:38 to justify simple ignorance. The argument of Dake on this point is a great one as he says, "In the name of the Lord Jesus simply means, 'by the authority of' the Lord Jesus, but how He authorized is recorded in Mt. 28:19."[24]

There is something unique about this church, which, when we understand it, will be clear why it was the first church and is so important for the church today. Note likewise:

> Of all the cities mentioned in the New Testament that were visited by Paul, Ephesus is the only one that was also

---

23 Finis J. Dake, *Dake Annotated Reference Bible*, Dake Bible Sales, Inc.
24 Ibid.

addressed in the book of Revelation. According to Acts, Paul visited the city of Ephesus on both his second and third missionary journeys. On his second journey his visit was brief. Priscilla and Aquila (wife and husband) accompanied Paul to Ephesus.[25]

After this particular visit, Paul left Priscilla and Aquila to continue in ministry while he met with the Jews in the synagogue and then sailed from Ephesus to Caesarea. After he left Ephesus, Apollos of Alexandria, considered an eloquent man, mighty in Scripture, and fervent in the Spirit, spoke and taught diligently the things of the Lord, but he knew only the baptism of John. However, he was zealous about the Lord and spoke boldly in the synagogue, and his teachings got the attention of Aquila and Priscilla. "Whom when Aquila and Priscilla had heard, they took him unto them, and expounded unto him the way of God more perfectly" (Acts 18:26).

Apollos was burning with zeal, but like some of the saints in Ephesus when Paul first got there, he didn't know much about Christ but was quite knowledgeable about the baptism of John. It is apparent that he received the instructions of Priscilla and Aquila and was well accepted by the brethren because, on his leaving Ephesus, he was given a letter of reference that he be received in Achaia. The record shows that he had an effective ministry there. "When Apollos went to the region of Achaia, It probably means he went to the city of Corinth in the region of Achaia. From what Paul writes in 1 Corinthians, he apparently had a remarkable ministry there"[26]

---

25 Clyde E. Fant and Mitchell G. Reddish, *A Guide to Biblical Sites in Greece and Turkey:* (New York: Oxford University Press, 2003), 180.

26 Guzik, David. "Study Guide for Acts 18." Enduring Word. Blue Letter Bible. 7 Jul 2006. http://www.blueletterbible.org/Comm/guzik_david/StudyGuide_Act/Act_18.cfm (accessed February 12, 2013).

This can be verified in what Paul wrote concerning the division and carnality of the saints who were choosing whether they were for "Paul or Apollos" (1 Corinthians 1:12; 3:4). The apostle Paul also instructed Timothy to spend time in Ephesus and teach against fables and things that do not edify or increase godliness.

Although it is not certain when Paul commissioned Timothy to abide in Ephesus, it is believed that it could have been after Paul was released from prison and went to Asia and then to Macedonia as we see in 1 Timothy 1:3–4: "As I besought thee to abide still at Ephesus, when I went into Macedonia, that thou mightiest charge some that they teach no other doctrine. Neither give heed to fables and endless genealogies, rather than godly edifying which is in faith: so do."

The apostle gave credit to Onesiphorus, who was not ashamed of his ministry even when he was in prison in Rome. He told Timothy that Onesiphorus sought him out and continued to minister to and refresh him even when he was in chains. "The Lord grant unto him that he may find mercy of the Lord in that day: and in how many things he ministered unto me at Ephesus, thou knowest very well" (2 Timothy 1:18).

He also informed Timothy to be diligent to come to him, for Demas had forsaken him, having loved the world. This could only be seen as a trying and lonely time for Paul, though he was not ashamed of the gospel of Christ, which is the power of God unto salvation. At this time, the apostle continued to express to Timothy that Luke alone was with him at that time, and that he had sent Tychicus to Ephesus.

As seen here, Ephesus and the Ephesians have a great religious and historic background and also great recognition in ancient Asia Minor. Now it's time to see what the Lord will reveal and what will be discovered in these letters to the churches.

The Letter to Ephesus

The letter begins with Christ addressing the minister in charge, who was held in Christ's right hand and was accountable for the church and what happened in it. The first letter is also addressed to the most famous of the seven churches. Be reminded, as stated times before, that there were many more than seven churches in Asia Minor. However, whether Jesus chose seven because seven is the number of completion or because these seven churches fit the characteristics of the ecclesiastical church throughout the great parenthesis/church dispensation is not known.

What is known, however, is that all through the ages, the experiences of these churches are seen almost everywhere. According to some beliefs, these churches are types and shadows with great symbolism and span the whole life of the church from the beginning stages until the last days of a predicted apostasy.

> They picture the course of the Church Age from the first coming of Jesus Christ to His Second Coming. Now the average person that you will deal with will know nothing about "dispensational truth" and when you use such terms as "Tribulation," "Rapture," "Millennium," he won't have the slightest idea what you are talking about—this is because the average preacher in America today knows less about the Bible than a salt water fisherman knew about it 1900 years ago.[27]

"Unto the angel 'messenger' of the church of Ephesus write." (Revelation 2:1) Having already looked at who the angel of the church likely is,

---

27   Peter S. Ruckman, The Book of Revelation: (BB Bookstore, Pensacola, FL 1970), Loc. 714.

whether the pastor or some angelic being in charge of the oversight of the church, here is the introduction of Christ's letter: "These things saith he that holdeth the seven stars in his right hand."(Revelation 2:1) Immediately, it is clear that Christ is establishing his authority, power, and control, beginning with the leader of the church. He holds the seven stars in his right hand. Each of these stars represents one of these churches, and being held in Christ's right hand suggests that he has certain leverage and control over the leaders and the churches.

To be in Jesus' right hand also implies safety, security, and subordination, but it could also mean total destruction. God told Jeremiah to go to the potter's house and observe how he handles the clay on the potter's wheels. The clay that was marred in the potter's hand was made over into another vessel as seemed good to the potter. "O house of Israel, cannot I do with you as this potter? Saith the Lord, behold as the clay is in the potter's hand, so are ye in mine hand, O house of Israel" (Jeremiah 18:6). So to be told that you are in God's hand could be comforting or it could be terrifying. Not only did Christ tell the church that he holds the seven stars in his hand, he also identifies himself as he "who walketh in the midst of the seven candlesticks" (Revelation 2:2).

This is rather interesting, not that the church was unaware of the omnipresence of Christ, but to hear him say that he is the one who walks in the midst of the seven golden candlesticks is a spine-chilling reminder that he knows all that's happening. First of all, a golden candlestick suggests something that is beautiful and also precious. Do not forget that the candlesticks, according to chapter 1, represent the church. The angels or the stars speak of the leadership, and the candlestick speaks of the church. He walks in the midst of the candlesticks, so when he says he knows all that was going on in the church, they understood what he meant, not just from his attributes of omniscience and omnipresence, but by his presence and experience.

As a matter of fact, the church, the body of Christ, is his dwelling place, and he abides with his people. "For where two or three are gathered together in my name, there am I in the midst of them" (Matthew 18:20). Christ being in the midst of the church does not simply suggest observation but intimates his personal relationship and intimacy with his church.

> Christ is in an intimate manner present and conversant with his churches; he knows and observes their state; he takes pleasure in them, as a man does to walk in his garden. Though Christ is in heaven, he walks in the midst of his churches on earth, observing what is amiss in them and what it is that they want.[28]

Here comes the emphatic statement: "I know thy works!" This is a statement that would be heard by all the churches. The word used for "works" is "*er-gon*, which means to toil as an effort or occupation."[29] By implication, it is an act, deed, or labor. In other words, Christ is saying, "I know all that you are involved in. Nothing goes unnoticed. "The positive emphatic statement, 'I know thy works,' is the basis for His righteous appraisal of the church; both of its praiseworthiness and its blameworthiness. Their works included the whole scope of their conduct—the labors and their behavior."[30]

Not only does Christ know theirs and everyone else's works, physically and spiritually, he also knows the motives by which the work was and is being done. All things are open before the eyes of the Lord; his eyes are in every place, beholding the evil and the good. Jesus told Nicodemus, "Verily, verily, I say unto thee, we speak of

---

28 Matthew Henry, Commentary on the whole Bible: Vol. VI-Acts to Revelation. (Macdonald Publishing company, McLean, Virginia), 1123.

29 Brian Thomas Webb, Strong's Concordance for iPhone version 1.5.3, Copyright 2009.

30 White Wing Publishing House, *The Seven Churches of Asia*. "Know your Bible Series" (White Wing Publishing House and Press, Cleveland, Tennessee, 2002), 22.

what we do know, and testify that we have seen; and ye receive not our report" (John 3:11).

Paul reminds all builders to take heed how they build on the foundation that has been laid because every man's work will be tried by fire. "Christ keeps an account of every day's work, and every hour's work, his servants do for him, and their labour shall not be in vain in the Lord."[31] At times, a reminder is paramount to remain aware that God knows every man's works. Often when one intends to do the unthinkable and the unconscionable, it is because he forgets that God knows his works. Jesus not only knew the works of the church of Ephesus and the other churches; here he tells them that he also knows their labor.

Although *er-gon*, the word used for "works," also speaks of labor, the actual word that Jesus used for "labor" is *kop`os*, which means "a cut." By analogy, it means to toil, but it is derived from the word *kop`to*, a primitive verb which means "to chop," specifically, to beat the breast in grief—cut down, lament, and mourn. It also means reducing of strength, literally or figuratively.[32] By implication, it speaks of pain, labor, trouble, and weariness. This implies that Christ was not only looking at what they had done but also what they had been through. He was aware of their pain, sufferings, and weaknesses, not only physically but also spiritually because their spiritual decline and failure was now known.

> He knew their labor, mentioning them twice, but in different aspects (verse 2 and 3). There was the manual, physical labor in various activities; but principally, that which was required in the interest of the spiritual welfare of the saints and the

---

31 Matthew Henry, Commentary on the whole Bible: Vol. VI-Acts to Revelation. (Macdonald Publishing company, McLean, Virginia), 1124.

32 Brian Thomas Webb, Strong's Concordance for iPhone version 1.5.3, Copyright 2009.

community. These labors were shared by the pastor and the church. In verse three the context suggests a sort of labor resulting from things that were difficult and unpleasant; but they had expended this effort for Christ's name's sake. Considering the upcoming rebuke (verse 4), we must ask: Is it possible to labor for Christ's name's sake without a love He can accept? Apparently so, since Christ Himself says this church did it. The discussion under verse four below will examine this further. But now, as they heard this letter being read, they may have pondered the true motives they had had as they had labored. Perhaps other thoughts on the subject came to their minds, which Paul and others had said or written.[33]

Rest assured that God will never forget a man's works good or bad; neither will he forget his labor of love. "Therefore, my beloved brethren, be ye steadfast, unmovable, always abounding in the work of the Lord, forasmuch as ye know that your labour is not in vain in the Lord" (1 Corinthians 15:58).

Christ also expressed to the church that he knew their patience. Patience is a key element in a Christian's daily walk if he is to overcome the constant challenges he face from the enemy of his soul. Patience allows him to continue trusting the Lord even when things are not going well. The patience exercised by these saints was at least threefold: in their physical labor and pain, their emotional pain, and with those who were evil and false teachers. "There is a 'bearing patience' which God gives to endure the injuries and hurts that men inflict upon us, as well as the reproofs we deserve. Then there is a 'waiting patience,'

---

[33] White Wing Publishing House, *The Seven Churches of Asia*. "Know your Bible Series" (White Wing Publishing House and Press, Cleveland, Tennessee, 2002), 22.

that when we have done the will of God, we may wait on Him for the promise (Hebrews 10:36)."[34]

"Patience is a virtue" is a cliché, but it is real and works well here. The encouragement by James fits well here, too, as he tries to encourage the Jews scattered abroad: "My brethren, count it all joy when ye fall into divers temptations; knowing this, that the trying of your faith worketh patience. But let patience have her perfect work, that ye may perfect and entire, wanting nothing" (James 1:2–4).

When patience has done its perfect work, it helps those who exercised it to become perfect, having been processed. Everyone is called to be diligent but must also be patient. To be patient requires endurance, and to endure is to undergo without giving in. "Jesus knows what this church is doing right. They work hard for the Lord and they have godly endurance. Patience is the great ancient Greek word (*hupomone*), which means 'steadfast endurance.' In this sense, the church is rock solid."[35]

Paul told Timothy, "Thou therefore endure hardness as a good soldier of Jesus Christ" (2 Timothy 2:3). Now the Lord tells them that he understands how they "canst not bear them which are evil."(Revelation 2:2) The Ephesian church was well taught in the doctrine of Christ by Paul, Priscilla, Aquila, and many others who were well grounded in the faith. Because of that, they had little or no tolerance toward evil. They could not bear them who "are evil"; one wonders, then, if there was something specific about these people why Jesus said they were evil, a profound statement from the Master.

This was an uncommon expression that meant something more than just one who does evil; they *were* evil. If one is evil, doing evil is second nature to that person, meaning he can't help himself when

---

34 White Wing Publishing House, *The Seven Churches of Asia*, 23.
35 David Guzik. "Study Guide for Revelation 2." Enduring Word. Blue Letter Bible. 7 Jul 2006. http://www.blueletterbible.org/Comm/guzik_david/StudyGuide_Rev/Rev_2.cfm (accessed February 12, 2013).

it comes to the act of or involvement in evil. There are not many times that Jesus make statements like this, but he did when talking to his disciples in John: "Have I not chosen you twelve, and one of you is a devil?" (John 6:70). If you know the nature and character of Judas, it would not be alarming, as he was the one to whom Jesus made reference.

Now think about this: if the actions of these people were typical to that of Judas, consider the dark valley they were going through. They were not saying they couldn't bear those who were evil. Christ himself was making the statement.

The nature of those who Jesus said were evil bears mentioning due to the extent of evil the church was experiencing. With that said, it's not hard to see how overbearing it was for the church. They, however, were well aware of what was coming because of the warnings of Paul after calling the elders of the church and preparing them for these things. It is not surprising, however, that they heard but did not take heed, which is not atypical of the church today—ever learning but never coming to the knowledge of the truth.

He also instructed the elders to feed the church and prepare for division that would be caused by ideologues who were driven by their philosophical and heretical allegiance. "For I know this, that after my departing shall grievous wolves enter in among you, not sparing the flock. Also of your own selves shall men arise, speaking perverse things, to draw away disciples after them" (Acts 20:29–30). This is a warning of division and the development of evil in the church.

The people must have experienced it and showed their frustration. They had patience in suffering and pain, but they did not have patience or tolerance when it came to evil. The Lord commended them for this, but they fell short in many other things. Christ also brought to the attention of the church that he observed their approach to vetting those who said they were apostles but were like wolves in sheep's clothing. This is what he said, "And thou hast tried them which say they are apostles, and are not, and hast found them liars."(Revelation 2:2)

That was a disciplined approach taken by the church concerning the false apostles. The word *tried*, or "*pi-rad-zo*, means to test, to scrutinize, to examine, and to prove."[36] It would do the church some good today if it would develop that same approach in the scrutiny of the many so-called apostles that are developing in this time.

> The church today, like the Ephesian church then, must vigorously test those who claim to be messengers from God—especially those who say they are apostles, because deceivers will speak well of themselves. The greater the evil, the more deceptive its cloak.[37]

This would certainly cause some to have second thoughts when declaring their apostleship. But then again, if they gravitate to those in their circle and those who do the laying of hands, they would be good to go. However, when they get on the radio and television, their influence goes far, especially for those who have become enamored with the desire for one to tell them their future.

Sadly for the church of Ephesus, although it was warned of the coming challenges, it was not able to avoid them, however, it handled those things with principle and fortitude. It is unfortunate, however, that one could be faithful over ninety-nine things but just ignoring one thing or doing wrong could cause an absolute downfall. The church struggled in its infancy dealing with evil, heresy, and false teachers.

This sets the stage for what the church would experience throughout the centuries until now. For them, facing enormous opposition and numerous well-established religions, they had no

---

36 Brian Thomas Webb, Strong's Concordance for iPhone version 1.5.3, Copyright 2009.

37 David Guzik. "Study Guide for Revelation 2." Enduring Word. Blue Letter Bible. 7 Jul 2006. http://www.blueletterbible.org/Comm/guzik_david/StudyGuide_Rev/Rev_2.cfm (accessed February 12, 2013).

room to make anything slip. Steadfastness in the doctrine of Christ was the only thing they had to hold onto. They held onto integrity and discipline and were steadfast in opposition, endured hardship, and went to great lengths to identify false apostles who they concluded were liars.

John in his epistle advised believers, "Believe not every spirit, but try the spirits whether they are of God: because many false prophets are gone out into the world" (1 John 4:1; 2 Corinthians 11:12–14; 1 Thessalonians 5:21). It could have been Judaizers pretending to be apostles with the intent of proselytizing the young and vulnerable church or others rising up in the church, claiming superior inspiration or illumination. But again, Paul saw those grievous wolves coming into the church as mentioned in Acts 20 and warned the leaders to beware.

Christ's observation was that this church had a lot going for it, as it did a number of things right. But it could not hold onto the love and passion it once had. Combining that with all its commendations would make it next to a perfect church. The last thing he said to them before expressing his displeasure was

> And hast borne [*bas-tad-zo,* to lift, endure, bear or carry, or to declare] and hast patience [*hoop-om-on-ay,* cheerful or hopeful endurance, constancy, or waiting] and for my name's sake hast laboured [*kop-ee-ah-o,* to feel fatigue, by implication, to work hard, toil, or be wearied] (Galatians 6:9; 2 Thessalonians 3:13) and hast not fainted [*kam-no,* to tire, figuratively, to faint, or become sick]. They showed godly perseverance that we should imitate. By all outward appearances, this was a solid church that worked hard, had great outreach, and protected the integrity of the gospel.[38]

---

38 David Guzik. "Study Guide for Revelation 2." Enduring Word. Blue Letter Bible. 7 Jul 2006. http://www.blueletterbible.org/Comm/guzik_david/StudyGuide_Rev/Rev_2.cfm (accessed February 12, 2013).

It is hard to hear all those wonderful accolades and then immediately hear "nevertheless." But to the heartbreak of that fighting church, that was exactly what Jesus said to them in his letter. It's like someone said to you, "I have good news and bad news. Which one do you want to hear first?" A letter coming from Jesus with all the good things mentioned in verses 2–3 would lift the spirit and encourage the heart of any church and its leaders. However, that was very short-lived, if it had time to take on any life whatsoever. "Nevertheless [*allah*], I have somewhat against thee, because thou hast left [*afeeaymee,* forsaken, lay aside] thy first love [*agahpay,* affection or benevolence, the love-feast]."[39] "Nevertheless" implies that in spite of all you have done, this cannot be overlooked.

What could have caused them to leave their first love? "They left" means they walked away from it, laid it aside, and forsaken it. Following is a wonderful thought by David Guzik because Jesus told them to remember from whence they had fallen:

> The distinction between leaving and losing is important. Something can be lost quite by accident, but leaving is a deliberate act, though it may not happen suddenly. As well, when we lose something we don't know where to find it, but when we leave something, we know where to find it.[40]

Now this is a serious and major indictment against a church. Jesus the omniscient one sees not only the good and the bad. He sees them both. He sees defects, coldness, and shortcomings in his church and must go to great lengths to identify them and give instructions on how to fix them. That same thing can be seen in the church today where the fire and expression of love for God needs to be rekindled.

---

39 Brian Thomas Webb, Strong's Concordance for iPhone version 1.5.3, Copyright 2009.
40 David Guzik,

For many, the expressions of deep love for the Lord have become secondary and works and labor take precedent.

Sometimes some become so taken by what others are or are not doing that all they focus on is fixing things or correcting others while their expression of love for Christ is nonexistent. The expression of love, whether for God or toward one another, is paramount to the life and energy of the church.

Like the church of Ephesus, if all the saints are concerned about is what people are doing and saying, the doctrinal teachings and principles of the church and all the external and, at times, internal things that do not enhance love and relationship with God and man can very soon bring a church to a dormant status. "Thou hast left thy first love." As Matthew Henry says,

> Not left and forsaken the object of it, but lost the fervent degree of it that at first appeared. Observe, (1.) The first affections of men towards Christ, and holiness, and heaven, are usually lively and warm. God remembered the love of Israel's espousals, when she would follow him whithersoever he went. (2.) These lively affections will abate and cool if great care be not taken, and diligence used, to preserve them in constant exercise. (3.) Christ is grieved and displeased with his people when he sees them grow remiss and cold towards him, and he will one way or other make them sensible that he does not take it well from them.[41]

With all that the church had done, Christ was even more concerned with the lack or absence of their pure expression of love toward him and each other. He had given a new commandment in John 13:35:

---

41 Matthew Henry, Commentary on the whole Bible: Vol. VI-Acts to Revelation. (Macdonald Publishing company, McLean, Virginia), 1124.

"That ye love one another as I have loved you ... By this shall all men know that ye are my disciples, if ye have love one to another."

Step one in fixing what has gone wrong is to remember what things were like before.

> Remember [*mnemoneue*, to exercise memory, rehearse, recollect] therefore from whence thou art fallen [*ekpipto*, to drop away, to be driven out of one's course, become inefficient, or fail] and repent [*metanoeho*, to think differently or afterward, morally, to feel compunction].[42]

This is the anxiety arising from an awareness of guilt. Jesus' words are not simply suggesting that the church feel sorry, but that it goes in another direction. In other words, it needs to remember the days when its personal relationship with him and each other had priority over all. It appears that during this time the church was on fire, when the love of Christ was the central theme to their coming together. But over time, they were overwhelmed by false prophets and those who were evil.

They should have remembered when they hungered and thirsted after righteousness; when they used to enter the holy place of God's presence and spent quality time in prayer; when they were as excited as the woman at the well, ready to share their experience and invite others to come see Christ; and when they couldn't wait to spend time in fellowship and worship with other believers. These are crucial to a Christian's growth and stability and enables him to resist evil.

Christ actually threatened the church that if they did not make amends and get back to the meaningful love relationship with him and the body of Christ, they would be in grave danger. "Or else" is a

---

[42] Brian Thomas Webb, Strong's Concordance for iPhone version 1.5.3, Copyright 2009.

direct threat of a pending consequence. Christ is saying, If there are no changes after this letter, I will not send another one but will take direct steps in meting out the ramifications. Or else I will come unto you 'quickly" [*takh-oo*, shortly, without delay, suddenly, or readily][43] and will remove thy candlestick out of his place, except thou repent.

If and when he came, he would remove their candlestick, or lampstand. In the previous chapter, recall that the seven candlesticks represented the seven churches. If a candlestick is removed, that church is removed. One commentator suggests that he would "remove their light and His presence. When their lampstand is removed, they may continue as an organization, but no longer as a true church of Christ. It would be a church of *Ichabod,* where the glory is departed (1 Samuel 4:21)."[44]

A church where the light and presence of God is nonexistent is nothing but a meeting place filled with hypocrisy. The question might be, Can a church really labor for Christ's sake and not have a genuine love for him? Paul talked to Timothy about people "having a form of godliness, but denying the power thereof: from such turn away" (2 Timothy 3:5).

> Here was a congregation duly commended for its labors, yet warned of pending removal for a defective love. A little sober thought will remind us that we can be in love with our own "system"—our own planned procedures and cherished goals—more than with the Christ whose name continues to cling to our tongues![45]

---

43   Brian Thomas Webb.
44   David Guzik. "Study Guide for Revelation 2." Enduring Word. Blue Letter Bible. 7 Jul 2006. http://www.blueletterbible.org/Comm/guzik_david/StudyGuide_Rev/Rev_2.cfm (accessed February 12, 2013).
45   White Wing Publishing House, *The Seven Churches of Asia.* "Know your Bible Series" (White Wing Publishing House and Press, Cleveland, Tennessee, 2002), 29.

If Christ moves the candlestick from a church, it would be left with only a form of godliness. Christ rebuked the scribes and the Pharisees, "Ye hypocrites, well did Esaias prophesy of you, saying, This people draweth nigh unto me with their mouth, and honoureth me with their lips; but their heart is far from me" (Matthew 15:7–8).

There is yet one more commendation for this church: it hated the deeds of the Nicolaitans, who Christ said he also hated and that anyone in the Christian faith who understood the doctrines or deeds of the Nicolaitans ought also to hate them.

The Nicolaitans had a bad reputation both morally and in doctrinal beliefs. They sheltered themselves under the umbrella of Christianity, but their way of life was gross and immoral to the lowest degree. They were followers of Nicolas, a heretic, who more will be said about later. There are different descriptions of this group. All of them are either bad or worse; none are in line with Christian values and character.

> The word "Nicolaitan" is not a translation, but a transliteration, like "baptism" or "apocalypse." The Greek word "niko" means "to conquer" and "laon" means "common or ordinary people" (laity). Hence, "the doctrine of the Nicolaitans" (v. 15) means the doctrine of how to conquer the common people.[46]

The Nicolaitans will show up again in the church of Pergamos, where a closer look will be taken at some of what they did and taught.

The Nicolaitans were like some today who do not believe they are diverting from Christian principles but rather are just modernizing them and making them more acceptable to the common people. A good example of this was at a special service where a so-called, self-

---

46 George Grace. *The Study of Revelation:* (First Bible Baptist Church. Rochester, NY 2010), 30.

acclaimed prophet from the south was the guest speaker. From the introduction of his sermon, one could sense where he was going, as he placed himself on a pedestal above everybody else, making it clear to everyone that he hears at a higher level than everyone else. Therefore, he was the only source or conduit through which God would speak—at least at the highest level.

> Though thou hast declined in thy love to what is good, yet thou retainest thy hatred to what is evil, especially to what is grossly so. The Nicolaitans were a loose sect who sheltered themselves under the name of Christianity. They held hateful doctrines, and they were guilty of hateful deeds, hateful to Christ, and to all Christians; and it is mentioned to the praise of the church of Ephesus that they had a just zeal and abhorrence of those wicked doctrines and practices. An indifference of spirit between truth and error, good and evil, may be called charity and meekness, but it is not pleasing to Christ. Our Savior subjoins this kind commendation to his severe threatening, to make the advice more effectual.[47]

The church of Ephesus was again commended for their intolerance and hatred of the character and behavior of the Nicolaitans. When Jesus says to you that you hate what he hates, that is a great compliment. The word *hate* is a strong word that is not often used in relation to God or Christ. However, this group was so abominable that the best way to express the feeling toward them was hate. The Greek word Christ used for "hate" is "*mis-eh-o,* and it means to abhor or to find repulsive."[48] This is not the same as when God said, "Yet I loved Jacob,

---

[47] Matthew Henry, Commentary on the whole Bible: Vol. VI-Acts to Revelation. (Macdonald Publishing company, McLean, Virginia), 1124.

[48] Brian Thomas Webb.

and I hated Esau" (Malachi 1:2–3). Here, this is an idiom and speaks of preference.

God preferred Jacob above Esau because of his lifestyle and offering, but he did not refer to personal malice or bitterness against Esau. However, when Jesus says he hated the deeds of the Nicolaitans, he means he detested them. According to David Guzik,

> These are powerful words in that they come from our Savior who is so rich in love. Whoever exactly the Nicolaitans were, and whatever they did and taught, we learn something from Jesus' opinion of them. We learn that the God of love hates sin, and wants His people to also hate sin.[49]

There is broad consensus that the Nicolaitans were from Nicolas, one of the first deacons ordained in the early church, who was a proselyte but later became doctrinally corrupt. Another look will be taken later when discussing the church of Pergamos.

The final admonition, exhortation, and promise given to all who will hear and take heed is: "He that hath an ear, let him hear what the Spirit saith unto the churches" (Revelation 2:7a). This message is sent to the church of Ephesus but has a much broader appeal to all who will hear.

This specific letter came to the church by John, but the general message comes from the Spirit of God who searches the deep things of God and brings conviction to the heart of man. He is the revealer of secrets. "And when he is come, he will reprove the world of sin, and of righteousness, and of judgment" (John 16:8). There is a heavy price to pay by all who will not listen to the Spirit. The voice of the

---

49 David Guzik. "Study Guide for Revelation 2." Enduring Word. Blue Letter Bible. 7 Jul 2006. http://www.blueletterbible.org/Comm/guzik_david/StudyGuide_Rev/Rev_2.cfm (accessed February 12, 2013).

Spirit of God is the most important voice one needs to hear and listen to. Unfortunately for many churches, his voice is not being heard.

There are a surmountable number of churches that are bent toward their own agendas that do not fit with that of the Spirit, and if they listen to him, he will bring their plans and operation to a halt. God judges motives many times and not the end result, so everyone needs to pay attention to their motives in whatever they do. Two sons of Aaron were killed because they kindled unholy fire before the Lord and were consumed. They lighted the fire and burned incense, as was protocol, but their hearts and motives weren't right.

They were instructed to not kindle the fire because their motive was not to do honor to the Lord but to exercise their priestly privileges. God's response was to consume them because they offered strange fire before him. "And there went out a fire from the LORD, and devoured them, and they died before the LORD" (Leviticus 10:2). God's response was that he would not accept offerings where his holiness was not recognized. "Then Moses said to Aaron, this is what the Lord was speaking about when he said, all who serve me must respect my holiness; I will reveal my glory to my people. But Aaron remained silent." (Leviticus 10:3 GNT)[50]

It is risky and dangerous to trifle with the Lord. The bottom line is that God judges everyone on an individual basis. Whoever listens to the Spirit of God and does all the things this church did that were right will find himself in good standing with God. If he avoids doing the things they were reprimanded for—and continue doing those things they should have been doing and were found wanting—all will be well with him.

Leaving one's first love will be to the peril of that believer who falls into this category. "To him that *overcometh* will I give to eat of

---

50 Good News Translation, http://www.biblegateway.com/passage/?search=Leviticus%2010&version=GNT (accessed September 13, 2013).

the tree of life, which is in the paradise of God" (Revelation 2:7b, emphasis added). This is a prophetic promise from Christ himself. It would be good to consider that this is not for the ancient church alone but for churches of all times.

There will be a reward to him who perseveres and to him who subdues the Enemy. The word "*nik-ah-o* means to subdue, to conquer, prevail, or get the victory."[51] To him that overcomes, Christ promises to allow him to eat from the Tree of Life, which is in the paradise of God.

There is a twofold thought to digest here in this promise. First is the Garden of Eden, where God placed Adam and Eve, giving them access to the Tree of Life of which they would eat and live forever. But their disobedience caused them to lose access to the Tree of Life.

It was God's intention that man would eat from the tree of Life and live forever. But after man sinned, he deserved the consequences of sin. God knew that with Adam's knowledge of good and evil, he would find a way to access the Tree of Life, eat from it, and live forever, even though the sentence of death was pronounced on him. And the Lord said,

> Now the man is become as one of us, to know good and evil: and now, lest he put forth his hand, and take also of the tree of life, and eat, and live forever: therefore the LORD God sent him forth from the garden of Eden, to till the ground from whence he came. (Genesis 3:22–23)

Second is the prophetic thought of God's promise to restore the Tree of Life to its original purpose. Hence, Christ promises the overcomers that they would (in the future) return to Eden or be restored to what

---

[51] Brian Thomas Webb, Strong's Concordance for iPhone version 1.5.3, Copyright 2009.

Eden represented in the beginning. This was a great incentive for the church as a group and as individuals to accept this great promise.

> This is meant first in the eternal sense of making it to heaven, which was no small promise to a church that was threatened with the removal of Jesus' presence. It is also meant in the sense of seeing the effects of the curse rolled back in our own lives through walking in Jesus' redeeming love.[52]

The paradise of God, as described by the Greek word *par-ad-i-sos*, compares to the Hebrew word *par-dace*, which speaks of a park or an orchard that is known as a place of great beauty. Specifically, the word speaks of Eden, a place of future happiness.[53] Historically, this was a phrase used by the Jews for paradise; it was also used in Luke 16:22, referring to Abraham's bosom, the place where Lazarus found comfort and happiness, opposite the rich man who was in torment.

The promise to those who overcome the challenges of false prophets, heresy, and immoral behavior; those who hate the hierarchical domination and subjugation of the Nicolaitans, and those who would overcome the coldness of leaving their first love would reap the benefit of God's paradise. Christ told the thief on the cross, "Verily I say unto thee, today thou shalt be with me in paradise" (Luke 23:43).

This church, like all the others, are chosen because God knew that all throughout the history of the church there would be similar experiences and situations that would need to be addressed that the leaders/angels of the church must pay attention to in order to stay in line and in favor with what Christ desires for his church. Unfortunately,

---

52 David Guzik. "Study Guide for Revelation 2." Enduring Word. Blue Letter Bible. 7 Jul 2006.2013. http://www.blueletterbible.org/Comm/guzik_david/StudyGuide_Rev/Rev_2.cfm (accessed February 12, 2013).

53 Brian Thomas Webb, Strong's Concordance for iPhone version 1.5.3, Copyright 2009.

most leaders are either ignorant, having made themselves so to avoid conviction in their conscience, or have chosen to ignore the voice of the Spirit. However, all should be warned that disobeying the Spirit will be to one's peril and certainly carries with it eternal consequences.

This is just another reminder that God will hold accountable the angels of the church, or those who are given oversight of his church. This Ephesian church is one to look at keenly to see how God instructed them to return to the passion and affectionate love they once shared.

CHAPTER 5

The Church of Smyrna

The second letter Christ gave to John was for the church in Smyrna. This church stood about forty miles north of Ephesus and south of Pergamos. Smyrna, like Ephesus, was strategically located near the coastline and was commercially successful because of its harbor. It was located near the ancient city of Iona on the western coast of Asia Minor. *Easton's Bible Dictionary* says, "It is now the chief city of Anatolia, having a mixed population of about 200,000, of whom about one-third are professed Christians."[54]

This beautiful city also carries a rich history, but like most ancient cities and provinces, it has been through many, sometimes painful, changes, often by way of destruction and rebuilding.

---

54 Easton's Bible Dictionary, http://www.ccel.org/e/easton/ebd/ebd/T0003400.html#T0003462

A quick view of the historical background of Smyrna shows that its earliest settlement dates back to the third millennium. Some of the excavation records suppose that findings of the remains of houses could date back as early as the seventh century BCE. It also had religious persuasions that greatly affected the church and Christianity. One cannot forget that the world actually began in these Far Eastern countries; therefore, the foundation of the church and its future experiences have been laid in these early churches. This was important so as Christianity expanded into world, Christians everywhere would be cognizant of what to expect and therefore learn by their example that the church of Christ would suffer for his cause. Persecution and suffering are not new to the church and will continue until Christ comes back.

If Christ's sufferings are examples for the church, what he said to the women who were weeping for him on the day of his crucifixion should prepare his followers for worse things: "Daughters of Jerusalem, weep not for me, but weep for yourselves, and your children … For if they do these things in a green tree, what shall be done in the dry?" (Luke 23:28–31).

It is not by chance that God found churches and people to use as examples both in the Old Testament and the early New Testament, leading up to these last days. Rightly, Christ has encouraged his saints not to be afraid of what they will go through in life, especially as his followers, because he foreknew the physical, mental, emotional, and spiritual battles they would encounter for his name's sake.

The church of Smyrna is another great example of Christian suffering and perseverance in the face of adversity, as Smyrna was a hot spot for Christian challenges. "In the 7th century a temple to Athena was built. This temple was destroyed around 600 B.C.E. by

King Alyattes of Lydia when he captured the city."[55] The previous destruction didn't dissuade the courageous religious people of Smyrna, who were determined to have that temple, so they rebuilt it. But unfortunately it was destroyed again by the Persians around 480 BC, as the suffering of this church continued.

Religious fanaticism and idol worship became a major factor in Smyrna. We will see the impact when we look at the letter Christ wrote to the church concerning what they went through because of their faith. This city was either lenient or unable to prevent different sects from establishing their religions by building and dedicating temples to various people. There was a temple built to the Mother Goddess and a temple built to the goddess Roma because the city wanted to show its loyalty to Rome.

> The city's loyalty to Rome was evidenced by its construction of a temple to the goddess of Roma in 195 B.C.E. the first city in Asia Minor to do so. Soon after the beginning of the 1st century B.C.E., Smyrna came under the control of the Roman providence of Asia. Smyrna was a major center for the imperial cult. In 23 B.C.E. the city was granted the privilege of building a temple to the emperor Tiberius. Later, it added temples to Hadrian and Caracalla. Various other buildings from Roman period are mentioned: a theater and a stadium on the slopes of Mt. Pagus, a silo built by Hadrian near the harbor, a commercial agora near the harbor, and a state agora. After a major earthquake extensively damaged the city in 178 C.E., Smyrna was able to rebuild due to help from the emperor Marcus Aurellus. During the Arab raids of the 7th century, the city was damaged but not destroyed.

---

55   Clyde E. Fant and Mitchell G. Reddish, *A Guide to Biblical Sites in Greece and Turkey* (New York: Oxford University Press, 2003), 318.

> Subsequently centuries saw Smyrna under the control of Seljuk Turks, Byzantine rulers, crusaders, and Ottoman Turks.[56]

There were many other notable buildings like stadiums, state agoras, and much more. These did not come easy. It is hard to imagine a city going through what Smyrna did and survive. There was something special and attractive about this city, as everyone wanted to be there.

> It was one of the most prosperous cities of Asia. With typical Chamber of Commerce and humility the city fathers called it "the pride of Asia." There was a hill named the Pagos back of the city, and around the crest of that hill a number of pagan temples, forming a rough circle, had been erected.[57]

Because of the formation of these temples on the hillside backdrop of Smyrna, it was also called "the Crown of Asia." The city had been through so much, and it seems that the church took on the same challenges. However, amidst the many destructions, "the city was re-founded by Alexander the Great, who was instructed in a dream to establish a new city on Mt. Pagus (now the site of the Kadifekale, or 'Velvet Fortress')."[58]

There is an untold number of events leading up to Christ's choosing Smyrna as one of the seven churches to receive a letter from him by the hand of John. The history of Christian suffering goes runs deep and goes far back.

---

56 Clyde E. Fant and Mitchell G. Reddish, *A Guide to Biblical Sites in Greece and Turkey* (New York: Oxford University Press, 2003), 319.

57 Vernon J. McGee. *The Seven Churches of Asia Minor* (Part 1). http://www.ldolphin.org/cleanpages/rev02.html, 20. (accessed May 7, 2013).

58 Clyde E. Fant and Mitchell G. Reddish, *A Guide to Biblical Sites in Greece and Turkey* (New York: Oxford University Press, 2003), 318.

The church of Smyrna was considered "The Persecuted Church that Prevailed" because of the persecution and martyrdom many of the early Christians experienced in that city. As will be seen later, Christ didn't accuse or reprimand this church of any wrongdoing or misconduct. The letter written to Smyrna was also the shortest of the seven letters; however, it never lacked in content.

As far back as the first century, documents indicate that there was a Jewish community in Smyrna, although it is uncertain when Christianity was actually established. However, Christianity then, like now, appears to be the most vulnerable, innocent, and yet most targeted. "Yea, and all that will live godly in Christ Jesus shall suffer persecution" (2 Timothy 3:12). Probably because the Christians were less aggressive and preached Christ, they became a prime target for their opposition—those who by virtue of their religious conviction would kill in the name of their God. Smyrna will forever be remembered in Christian history as one of the seven churches to which Christ sent a letter.

In the second century, all eyes were on Smyrna. "The city earned a spot in Christian history, however, when Ignatius, bishop of Antioch in Syria stopped at Smyrna while being transported to Rome for execution around 107 C.E. While there, Ignatius met with Christian leaders from Asia Minor and while at Smyrna."[59]

Even during his journey to face his death at Rome, Ignatius was still writing letters and sending them back to the church in Smyrna. One of his fellow laborers and ultimate fellow martyr, Polycarp, who was also a bishop in Smyrna, received a letter from him. There are some who believe that Ignatius and Polycarp were disciples of John the apostle, as these men laid down their lives for the cause of Christ and were examples for the church in Smyrna. Polycarp himself was

---

59 Clyde E. Fant and Mitchell G. Reddish, *A Guide to Biblical Sites in Greece and Turkey* (New York: Oxford University Press, 2003), 319.

burned at the stake in the stadium of Smyrna. Believed to have been a Christian from his childhood days, for unknown reasons, the Romans didn't kill him until he was passed four-score years.

> Smyrna had two characteristics which made life for the Christians a constant and continued peril. Smyrna was one of the great centers of Caesar worship. If we are to understand the peril and threat which was at the back of every Christian life when the book of Revelation was written, we must understand how Caesar worship arose and how it functioned. The problem of Rome was how to unify its vast Empire. The Roman Empire was a vast conglomeration of states and cities and nations and peoples and races covering the whole known world. Something was needed to unify and to integrate all varying elements in this huge mass. None of the extant religions was capable of being universalized. But one thing was capable of being universalized—the spirit of Rome itself.[60]

The Letter to Smyrna

This letter, like the others, is sent to the angel of the church, which has already been explained is the pastor or leader of the church, and the candlestick mentioned in chapter 1 is the church. "And unto the angel of the church in Smyrna write; these things saith the first and the last, which was dead, and is alive" (Revelation 2:8). When you look at how Christ addressed this church, you see that he was aware that they were experiencing great tribulation. It should not be strange,

---

60 William Barclay, *Letters to the Seven Churches*, (Westminster John Knox Press, Louisville, Kentucky, 2001), 16.

though hard to deal with, that this church went through the things it did. If it is a symbolic church, its name was intended by God himself.

The meaning of the word *smyrna* is "myrrh." While myrrh is a form of perfume, it has great symbolism if one looks at how it's often used in history. It is understood that in order to acquire the fragrance, one has to crush the myrrh, which is indicative of what the church was experiencing. It was part of the principal ingredient in the holy anointing oil mentioned in Exodus 30:23: "Take thou also unto thee principal spices, of pure myrrh five hundred shekels." Myrrh was also one of the three gifts the wise men brought to Mary and Joseph at the birth of Christ as mentioned in Matthew 2:11b: "And when they had opened their treasures, they presented unto him gifts; gold, frankincense, and myrrh."

Of course, these three gifts were significant in the life of Christ. The gold represented his deity. Frankincense represented his worship and adoration, the burning of which in the temple symbolized praise with its sweet smell into the nostrils of God. Myrrh represented his suffering and was also used for embalming. Suffering and death were associated closely with the church of Smyrna. Who best then to address this church but he who knew their works and tribulation?

This church had an enormous amount of similarities to Christ. As myrrh represented bitter suffering, Christ literally had this experience. "And when they come unto a place called Golgotha, that is to say, a place of a skull, They gave him vinegar to drink, mingled with gall: (bitter) and when he had tasted thereof, he would not drink" (Matthew 27:33–34).

Christ was lambasted, ridiculed, and tortured. He wore a crown of thorns and was beaten with many stripes, given his cross to carry, and ultimately crucified. The church of Smyrna typified the entire three-and-a-half years of Christ's ministry, so he could identify with their experiences like no other. He could identify with all that they went through and would go through. The church was poor, and Jesus, too, lived a life of humility.

For Christ to introduce himself as "the first and the last, which was dead, and is alive," (Revelation 2:8) he immediately reminds them of his eternal existence. He is before all things and will be after all things; from everlasting to everlasting he is God. This is in similar manner to how he introduced himself to John on the isle of Patmos. "I am the Alpha and Omega." (Revelation 1:8) He knows from eternity past to eternity future. Not only that, he reminded them of what he had been through and was still alive that day. Why was that significant? For Christ to say to a church where its people were tortured and martyred for his name's sake that he was dead and is now alive was designed to instill hope in them and to encourage and remind them of the resurrection and life after death. This was saying to them, "I know what you are going through. Remember, I have been through the same things, and look at me today. I was dead and am now alive."

> He thus reminded them that He had suffered and died for the Church because He loved it. He could be touched with the feeling of their infirmity because He was "in all points tempted as we were, yet without sin" (Hebrews 4:15). Now if they would willingly suffer with Him, they would also reign with him (2 Timothy 2:13).[61]

Christ's testimony of being alive has at least three components. One, "was dead" suggests that he was alive and then died, the reason for which was to pay the price for their redemption. The angel told Daniel, "Messiah would be cut off, but not for himself" (Daniel 9:26). Two, he was alive for their justification and was the testator. The will or testament is not in effect until the testator dies. After the testator dies, his last will and testament is executed by another, who sometimes

---

61 White Wing Publishing House, *The Seven Churches of Asia.* "Know your Bible Series" (White Wing Publishing House and Press, Cleveland, Tennessee, 2002), 43.

manipulates and alters the testator's will. But Jesus Christ would not allow alteration to his will. More so, he alone was holy and able to provide justification, so he came back to life to execute his own will and testament. Three, he's alive because he must advocate for the saints, or to speak on their behalf.

Christians cannot forget that Christ was and is victorious over death for their benefit. As a matter of fact, he told John that he had the keys of death and hell. As death couldn't hold him, the assurance to those who may die for him is that they would live again, and those who had lost loved ones by way of martyrdom should keep hope alive. The testimony of Job fits in this conversation as he exercised his confidence in the resurrection. "If a man die, shall he live again? All the days of my appointed time will I wait, till my change come" (Job 14:14).

Part of the Christian's journey is what he or she suffers for Christ by taking up the cross and following him. "For whosoever will save his life shall lose it: but whosoever shall lose his life for my sake and the gospel's, the same shall save it" (Mark 8:35). Part of what drives a Christian and keeps him or her going in the face of adversity is remembering what the apostle says: "For to me, to live is Christ, and to die is gain" (Philippians 1:21).

It is now time for Christ not only to tell the church of Smyrna that he is alive from the dead but also to let them know clearly his fundamental reason for sending them this letter. As he did with the other churches, he made it clear that his awareness of the work and works of the churches was unquestionable. Unlike everybody else who needed a report on what had taken place in their absence, Christ is never absent. He is perfect in all his ways and transcends time and space. He is not governed by spatial limitations, nor is he an object with finite flexibility.

His being God, the creator of all things and who knows all things, he sits high and looks low. "Neither is there any creature that is not made manifest in his sight: but all things are naked and opened unto the eyes of him with whom we have to do" (Hebrews 4:13). God knows and sees everything as they happen. Furthermore, he knows what will happen even before we do. One of Christ's great attributes is his omniscience, which he displayed while he was here in the flesh.

If one recalls some of the demonstrations of the omniscience of Christ, one would know that it is time to shrink and shrivel when Jesus declares, "I know thy works!" Here are a couple of instances when Christ demonstrated his omniscience before we look more at the letter to Smyrna. This might help you better understand what it meant to the churches when Jesus said that he knew their works.

Nathaniel, out of his curiosity, came to see Jesus after Philip invited him, but Nathaniel was a bit skeptical about Philip having found him who Moses and the prophets wrote about, Jesus of Nazareth, the son of Joseph. Nathaniel wondered if any good thing could come out of Nazareth, but Philip told him to come and see. When Jesus saw him, he declared, "Behold an Israelite indeed, in whom is no guile." Astounded, Nathaniel asked Jesus, "Whence knowest thou me?" Jesus' response was mind blowing to him: "Before Philip called you, when you were under the fig tree, I saw you" (John 1:45–48). He replied, "Rabbi (master), you are the Son of God, the King of Israel. He knew the heart of Judas at the table" (John 13:11). In another instance, in John 21:17, Peter told Christ, "Lord, thou knowest all things; and thou knowest that I love thee."

More instances of Jesus demonstrating his omniscience can be found in Matthew 12:25; 22:18; Luke 6:8; and Revelation 2:23.

So going back to the church, Jesus saying, "I know thy works," has more credibility than could be comprehended by finite human understanding. One would imagine that "I know thy works" was scary to hear by this poor, tried, and suffering church. But before they could digest the idea, or begin to evaluate what was next, Jesus said, "and tribulation," which immediately set the tone for the rest of this letter.

The word that Jesus used for tribulation is *thlip-sis,* which speaks of pressure, literally or figuratively. It also means to be afflicted, to go through anguish, to be burdened, persecution, and trouble.[62] These were the things that identified the church at Smyrna. This church had seen more than its share of martyrdom, if that term could be used justifiably. It is believed that at the time John took this letter to the church of Smyrna that Polycarp was the angel of the church. He was also a disciple of John and was martyred in his eighties, though he defended the Christian faith from childhood. "John's disciple, Polycarp, even at the time of writing, may have been the 'angel' of the church. He died a martyr's death in 155 AD as very advanced age, testifying that he had known and served the Lord for 86 years."[63]

If you notice, Smyrna is one of the two churches that Christ did not rebuke in his letters. The other is the church of Philadelphia, which will be looked at later. However, Smyrna is the church that had suffered the most and therefore warranted Christ's recognition of their tribulation. Did they suffer because they stood up for Christ and refused to worship idols or recognize other gods? Did they suffer tribulation because they were poverty-stricken? One might say some of both, but God in his infinite wisdom and power, who knew their works and tribulation, was ready to give them hope.

The church's persecution grew as idol worshiping expanded, and it got even worst when the Roman emperor demanded worship under the disguise of "lord." The pressure intensified for the Christians, and their persecution became unbearable. It was under the rule of Domitian that John was exiled to Patmos. Once the emperor gained a foothold, what was considered free-will worship was now required as he constantly tightened his grip like a vice. Domitian began his domination after he deified himself and assumed the title of lord

---

62 Brian Thomas Webb, Strong's Concordance for iPhone version 1.5.3, Copyright 2009.

63 Jim Combs. *Rainbows from Revelation:* (Tribune Publishers, Springfield MO, 1994), 31.

and god. Driven by his ego, he took the demand for recognition to another level.

Domitian also prided himself as the reformer of religion and morality. "Emperor Worship had begun as spontaneous demonstration of gratitude to Rome; but toward the end of the first century, in the days of Domitian the final step was taken and Caesar worship became compulsory."[64] The requirement was that once each year the Roman citizens pay homage to Caesar. A similar scenario occurred when Nebuchadnezzar invited the people of the provinces of Babylon to the dedication of his golden image.

Once they were gathered and the iron gates of Babylon were closed, he made his decree, not simply for the dedication of the image, but so the people would bow down and worship the image. The Hebrew boys were later thrown into the fiery furnace because they refused to bow to this idol (Daniel 3).

During this time of the Roman emperor's demands, the people would not need to constantly worship but would be given a certificate to prove that they had done their religious duties and had worshipped the emperor.

> All the Christians had to do was to burn that pinch of incense, say "Caesar is Lord," receive their certificate, and go away and worship as they pleased. But that is precisely what the Christians would not do. They would give no man the name Lord; that name they would keep for Jesus Christ and Jesus Christ alone. They would not even formerly conform (Barclay).[65]

---

64 David Guzik. "Study Guide for Revelation 2." Enduring Word. Blue Letter Bible. 7 Jul 2006. http://www.blueletterbible.org/Comm/guzik_david/StudyGuide_Rev/Rev_2.cfm (accessed February 12, 2013).

65 Ibid

Of course this led to Christians being vilified, ostracized, disqualified from routine trading, tortured, and sometimes killed.

As stated previously, John was exiled to Patmos during the reign of Domitian. If you notice, this had been going on for a long time because John spent about thirteen years on Patmos. So the letter offering a sense of comfort was appropriately delivered to the church by the hands of John. This did not go unnoticed by Christ. As said before, the first thing Christ said to the church of Smyrna, after letting them know that he knew their works, was that he also knew their tribulation.

> The Smyrna church was told in v. 10, "fear none of those things which thou shalt suffer," but to be "faithful unto death," not until death. They were to remain faithful and not recant when called upon to face the Martyr's death ... Historically this is the persecuted church of 200–325 AD. During this time, the pagan government of Rome aggressively persecuted the Christian church.[66]

"I know thy poverty," Jesus says, which implies that they were at the low place of beggary, as the word *pto-khi-ah* suggests. This is how they were looked upon and possibly how they felt among themselves, apparently because they were ostracized by the Roman emperor. But the message from Christ was "But thou art rich!" You will find no comparison with the church in Laodicea that thought it was rich and wanting nothing but really was poor, naked, and blind. Smyrna got the good news from Christ; they were actually rich. "Poor in

---

66 George Grace. *The Study of Revelation:* (First Bible Baptist Church. Rochester, NY 2010), 21.

temporals, but rich in spirituals—poor in spirit, and yet rich in grace. Their spiritual riches are set off by their outward poverty."[67]

They were not only poor; they were living in poverty. The story of Lazarus in Luke 16 would have given them reason to persevere. The beggar died and was carried into Abraham's bosom, while the rich man died and was buried. In all of that, they held their integrity and did not compromise their faith. There was a sect that professed Judaism, but their actions put that into question. Jesus described them as pretending to be Jews, but their gathering was "the synagogue of Satan."(Revelation 2:9) In other words, their gathering was a meeting place for the Devil. They pretended to be Jews but blasphemed the name of God and served Satan. It is not strange to hear that there was a synagogue of Satan. He has been trying to copy everything that Christ has done but has always come up short. Today there are more worshippers of Satan than ever before, and he and his agents are desiring to destroy those who are God's. But God will allow him only so much and no more.

> For no temptation (no trial regarded as enticing to sin), [no matter how it comes or where it leads] has overtaken you *and* laid hold on you that is not common to man [that is, no temptation or trial has come to you that is beyond human resistance and that is not [b]adjusted and [c] adapted and belonging to human experience, and such as man can bear]. But God is faithful [to His Word and to His compassionate nature], and He [can be trusted] not to let you be tempted *and* tried *and* assayed beyond your ability *and* strength of resistance *and* power to endure, but with the temptation He will [always] also provide the way

---

67 Matthew Henry, Commentary on the whole Bible: Vol. VI-Acts to Revelation. (Macdonald Publishing company, McLean, Virginia), 1124.

out (the means of escape to [d]a landing place), that you may be capable *and* strong *and* powerful to bear up under it patiently. (1 Corinthians 10:13b)[68]

An evaluation of what the church of Smyrna had been through would cause one to think it was more than enough. However, that was not how Christ prophetically declared it to them. There was more to come, and worse! "Fear none of those things which thou shalt suffer" (Revelation 2:10) was a futuristic statement.

The irony is that they were being commended for what they had been through and were told at the same time to get ready for more. The Devil would have some of them cast into prison that they may be tried, but he would still be limited to what he would be able to inflict on God's faithful children. "Ten days" suggests a limited time; however, there is no consensus on exactly what this means, whether it is literal, metaphorical, prophetic, or symbolic.

David Guzik, in his commentary on the church of Smyrna, gave five scenarios from different commentators in view of the "ten days" Christ mentioned. These vary quite a bit, so it will take a wealth of personal conviction to make a conclusion. Here are two of the references he noted.

> i. Some think that John really means ten years of persecution. "As the days in this book are what is commonly called prophetic days, each answering to a year, the ten years tribulation may denote ten years of persecution; and this was precisely the duration of the persecution under Diocletian, during which all the Asiatic Churches were grievously afflicted" (Clarke) ii. Others think that John really means

---

68 The Amplified Bible, http://www.biblegateway.com/passage/?search=1+Corinthians+10&version=AMP. (accessed September 13, 2013).

persecution over the reign of ten Roman Emperors. "The first under Nero, A.D. 54; the second under Domitian, A.D. 81; the third under Trajan, A.D. 98; the fourth under Adrian, [Hadrian] A.D. 117; the fifth under Septimus Severus, A.D. 193; the sixth under Maximin, A.D. 235; the seventh under Decius, A.D. 249; the eight under Valerian, A.D. 254; the ninth under Aurelian, A.D. 270; the tenth under Diocletian, A.D. 284 (White, cited in Walvoord)."[69]

These are only a couple of the many views on this statement. However, from whichever angle this is viewed, the bottom line is, one, many in the church would be imprisoned and face great tribulation or severe persecution; and two, it would be for a set time known, designed, or just allowed by God.

Unfortunately, this was not unfamiliar territory for them. They had been through many trials and persecution that caused Christ to remind them that he knew of their tribulation. Christ admonished them, "Be thou faithful unto death," which suggested not giving up in the process.

The promise to those who were faithful unto death was the crown of life, which is the martyr's crown. This promise is guaranteed, for the language Jesus used confirms it: "I will give thee a crown of life," which removes the chance of the second death. The crown of life is a badge of royalty and a symbol of honor that is reserved for the faithful. "Blessed is the man that endureth temptation, for when he is tried, he shall receive the crown of life, which the Lord hath promised to them that love him" (James 1:12).

Finally, to the church of Smyrna, there is a similar conclusion: "He that hath an ear, let him hear what the Spirit saith unto the

---

[69] David Guzik. "Study Guide for Revelation 2." Enduring Word. Blue Letter Bible. 7 Jul 2006. http://www.blueletterbible.org/Comm/guzik_david/StudyGuide_Rev/Rev_2.cfm. (accessed February 12, 2013).

churches, 'He that overcometh shall not be hurt of the second death'" (Revelation 2:11). This is an interesting statement of comfort to the church. Shall not be "hurt," *ad-ee-keh-o*, to be unjust, to do wrong, socially or physically, to injure, or suffer.[70]

> Those who overcome in Jesus will never be hurt by the second death. The second death is hell, the lake of fire (Revelation 20:14 and 21:18). Though Satan has threatened and attacked their life, Jesus promises His overcomers that death is conquered for them.[71]

The knowledge of God's faithfulness brought comfort to the saints at Smyrna, knowing that God had always kept his promises. The apostle made it plain to the Hebrews: "Let us hold fast the profession of our faith without wavering; (for he is faithful that promised)" (Hebrews 10:23). He guards his promises and is self-existent and immutable. The church had a lot to overcome, which was why it was so important for them to be reminded by Christ of the great reward that awaited those who overcame.

It is hard to imagine from the outside or from far away what the saints of Smyrna had been through. They were not only up against other gods and idol worshippers, but they were also up against the Jews who hated them and would even side with the Romans, Caesar's faithful followers, or the Gentiles, who were their enemies, if it meant more persecution for the Christians. This was the means by which Polycarp had died.

The Jews were strong in Smyrna; they had the ear of the authorities. Such was their envenomed bitterness that they would even plead

---

70 Brian Thomas Webb, Strong's Concordance for iPhone version 1.5.3, Copyright 2009.

71 David Guzik, http://www.blueletterbible.org/Comm/guzik_david/StudyGuide_Rev/Rev_2.cfm. (accessed February 12, 2013).

concern for the pagan gods, and even join with the hated Gentiles, if by so doing they could bring death to the Christians. It was a threat like that in Smyrna hung over the Christian church.[72]

The saying, "The enemy of my enemy is my friend," has been well played out in these experiences of the church. This threat is extant today in various parts of the world, though in most places of the Western world it is virtually nonexistent. People in places like India, Pakistan, Afghanistan, and Africa, to name a few, are still tortured and killed because of their faith. But many are kept by the same promise Christ made to the church of Smyrna. Those who overcome will be eternally rewarded. It should be noted that "to overcome" does not mean one will not die in the process.

The apostle Paul made it clear in two very profound statements. First, "We are confident, *I say*, and willing rather to be absent from the body, and to be present with the Lord" (2 Corinthians 5:8). And second, "According to my earnest expectation and my hope, that in nothing I shall be ashamed, but that with all boldness, as always, so now also Christ shall be magnified in my body, whether it be by life or by death. For me to live is Christ, and do die is gain" (Philippians 1:20–21).

> There were Christians in Smyrna who were men of such heroic calibre that the word of the Risen Christ to them was a word of unadulterated praise. In a city where the splendor of heathen worship might well have suffocated the life of the Christian church, in a city where the pride of men looked on the humble Christians with arrogant contempt, in a city where every Christian was between the devil of the demands of Caesar worship and the deep sea of

---

72 William Barclay, 21.

Jewish slander and malignity, there were Christians who were faithful unto death.[73]

It doesn't matter what the dispensation is; it doesn't matter what the persecution is or has been; it doesn't matter how many have failed, given up, or died, God will always have a remnant who will keep fighting and make it through the storm. And there is one thing to be assured of: God rewards faithfulness.

---

73 William Barclay, 21.

CHAPTER 6

THE CHURCH OF PERGAMOS

Pergamos, as mentioned in Revelation as the third church to receive a letter from Christ, was located north of Smyrna and was the third most western from Patmos of the churches. There is little known of the ancient early history of Pergamum prior to the Hellenistic period. Pergamos was somewhat in the dark without recognition until it was under the control of Alexander the Great, who is also known as Alexander of Macedonia. Alexander overthrew the Persian Empire, but his kingdom was dismantled after his death and became a fragmented kingdom of four smaller ones, which did not stand the test of time.

The Greeks established themselves after his death and established the Hellenistic age where Greek culture dominated Pergamos and surrounding areas until the conquest of Rome.

From the breakup of Alexander's empire there arose numerous realms, including the Macedonian, the Seleucid, and the Ptolemaic, that served as the framework for the spread of Greek (Hellenic) culture, the mixture of Greek with other populations, and the fusion of Greek and Oriental elements.[74]

Pergamos was infested with a diversity of cultures, religious sects, and idol worship. The adaptation of the church of Pergamos to these various practices earned it the name the compromising church. It had become the first city to build a temple to Caesar. It was surrounded by pagan culture and eventually affected the church, as will be seen in Jesus' letter. It was also the political capital of Asia Minor. It is no wonder it was named Pergamos, which means "fortified."

Pergamos was fortified and was known for its intrepid politics and religions. "Pergamum enjoyed a rich and a varied religious history. Temples to Athena, Zeus, Hera, Dionysus, Demeter, and Asclepius were among many temples situated in the city. In addition, the city was a major center of the imperial cult of Asia Minor."[75]

There is no excuse for a church to become blemished by the world and to partake in external influences and idol worship. However, it would take a lot of integrity in Christ to persevere during the inundation of religious cults that pervaded the city. This, of course, prompted Christ to call where the church sat as where "Satan's seat is." This is another example of what the church faces today and what Christ expects of it in the face of adversity and satanic forces.

The church's ability to survive depends on its dedication to Christ and adherence to the doctrines of his grace. "Corrupt morals

---

74 Encyclopaedia Britannica. http://www.britannica.com/EBchecked/topic/260307/Hellenistic-Age. (accessed August 18, 2013).

75 Clyde E. Fant and Mitchell G. Reddish, *A Guide to Biblical Sites in Greece and Turkey* (New York: Oxford University Press, 2003), 275.

prevailed, associated with the many idols. Morally contaminating idolatrous idolatrous rites were frequent and varied."[76]

Pergamos is not referred to often in Scripture; as a matter of fact, it is only mentioned twice, once in Revelation 1:11 when Christ commissioned John to write and once in chapter 2 when the letter was actually written. It could, therefore, be said that if there was a church that did not warrant Christ's attention, Pergamos would not have been recorded in Holy Scripture. However, because of the letter sent to it, and because of its characteristics and how it relates to the church today, it will be forever remembered.

> Pergamum is mentioned indirectly in 1 Maccabees 8:8, in a passage that describes Roman conquests in the ancient world. After telling of the defeat of Antiochus III by the Romans, the passage states that the Romans took some of the former territories of Antiochus and gave them "to King Eumenes" a reference to Eumenes II of Pergamum and his acquisition of additional lands after the defeat of Antiochus III at Magnesia in 189 B.C.E.[77]

An interesting scenario took place over the centuries in Pergamos as Christianity grew and paganism declined—some of the prominent places of pagan worship were used for Christians to worship. For some Christians, there would be a form of vindication for just having access to these formidable places. "Temples to idols became church edifices. In 431 at the council of Ephesus, the title 'Mother of God'

---

[76] White Wing Publishing House, *The Seven Churches of Asia*. "Know your Bible Series" (White Wing Publishing House and Press, Cleveland, Tennessee, 2002), 56.

[77] Clyde E. Fant and Mitchell G. Reddish, *A Guide to Biblical Sites in Greece and Turkey* (New York: Oxford University Press, 2003), 276.

was applied to the Virgin Mary, an act which ended Diana worship, but instituted a new female figure for adoration."[78]

The church, however, did not live up to Christ's expectation, as they corrupted themselves with the doctrine of the Nicolaitans and some of them adopted the doctrine of Balaam.

The Letter to Pergamos

The letter, as were the previous ones, was sent to the "angel of the church" of Pergamos. As stated earlier, Pergamos means "fortified," which speaks of the nature and structural development of the city but not necessarily the standing of the church. Christ introduced himself as "He which hath the sharp sword with two edges." This ought to be a scary introduction for a church, especially when conscience says they were obviously behaving contrary to the doctrines of grace. John's description of Christ when he heard him speak in Revelation 1:16 when he introduced himself is as follows: "And out of his mouth went a sharp sword: and his countenance was as the sun shineth in his strength."

John's description of how Christ looked and sounded when he saw him is justified in Christ's introduction to the church. What he was about to say to this church is parallel to what the apostle said to the Hebrews: "For the word of God is living and active, sharper than any two-edged sword, piercing to the division of soul and of spirit, of joints and of marrow, and discerning the thoughts and intentions of the heart." (Hebrews 4:12 ESV).[79]

---

[78] Jim Combs. *Rainbows from Revelation:* (Tribune Publishers, Springfield MO, 1994), 32.

[79] English Standard Version ESV. http://www.biblegateway.com/passage/?search=Hebrews%204&version=ESV. (accessed September 13, 2013).

Christ was ready to cut to the heart and soul of the church of Pergamos for their failure to do right. The Word of God will cut left and right and will not return to him void, whether by God himself, the Holy Spirit, or preachers who are given the authority to declare, "Thus saith the Lord, I know thy works,'" as he did concerning the other churches. The beginning of the indictment of this church is where they dwell. "Thou dwellest even where Satan's seat is." (Revelation 2:13) This is an intriguing statement, and there are many beliefs concerning it. It is believed that Satan's seat was first located in Babylon but moved its headquarters to Pergamos.

> In this Message Pergamos is spoken of as "Satan's Seat." When Attalus III, the Priest-King of the Chaldean Hierarchy, fled before the conquering Persians to Pergamos, and settled there, Satan shifted his capital from Babylon to Pergamos. At first he persecuted the followers of Christ, and Antipas was one of the martyrs.[80]

It is interesting and complicated to say the least that a church was located where Satan's seat was, yet they held fast the name of the Lord and had not denied his name. They did not abnegate or disavow his name even when they were persecuted severely. Christ told the church at Smyrna to "be faithful unto death," (Revelation 2:10) and that's exactly what Antipas did, whose name actually means "against all." Christ calls him his faithful martyr. According to Finis Dake in his Bible commentary on Antipas, he was "An unknown Christian who became known by his martyrdom for Christ. There is a book called The Acts of Antipas, which makes him the bishop of Pergamos

---

[80] Clarence Larkin, The Book of Revelation: (Rev. Clarence Larkin Estate, 1919), 22.

and states that he was put to death by being enclosed in a burning brazen bull."[81]

It took a lot of will to go through tribulation and even death for your comrades and yet hold onto the name of the Lord. However, the next statement following this great commendation was unpleasant to the ear. "But I have a few things against thee." (Revelation 2:14) They held onto the name but diverted from the doctrines. One would consider that the height of hypocrisy, trying to have it both ways or to disguise the lifestyle by holding onto the name. The first thing Christ had against them was there were some of them who held the doctrine of Balaam.

There is a lot that can be said about the doctrine of Balaam. As mentioned in Numbers 22–25, Balaam is said to have practiced sorcery and divination. It is believed that he was once a good prophet of God but became corrupt when he placed gifts and sorcery above the command of the Lord. "Balaam was a prophet (2 Peter 2:16). Some brand him as 'typical hireling prophet.' Others consider him to have once been a prophet of the true God, but had himself taken up sorcery and divination, more or less 'juggling' the two ministries."[82]

The doctrine of Balaam also included teaching and influencing Israel to commit whoredom, to put a stumbling block in their way, to cause them to eat things offered unto idols, and to commit fornication. His intent was that by their sinning against God, he would himself curse them and therefore grant Balak his desire. Read the whole story in Numbers 22–25.

---

[81] Finis Dake. Dake annotated Reference Bible, 287, b.
[82] White Wing Publishing House, *The Seven Churches of Asia*. "Know your Bible Series" (White Wing Publishing House and Press, Cleveland, Tennessee, 2002), 61.

The Nicolaitans

Another thing against this church was that some were holding to the doctrines of the Nicolaitans. The Nicolaitans, whose name means "to conquer the people," were followers of Nicolaus, a heretic who was believed to have been a proselytized Gentile who once served as a deacon but fell into heresy and immorality. They were considered to be a sect of Gnostics who believed, practiced, and taught immorality—an impure group that fell from the doctrine of truth and believed that it was not adultery if one had more than one wife. They ignored the doctrine of adultery and fornication, which also led them to further error by indulging in idol worship and eating meat offered to idols.

The Nicolaitans seem to have made themselves prevalent among the churches, at least among the saints of Ephesus and again at Pergamos. The great difference between the two churches was that the church of Ephesus hated the deeds of the Nicolaitans while some at Pergamos held to the doctrines of the Nicolaitans. Note: The deeds at Ephesus, something that they practiced, had become doctrine at Pergamos and part of what some believed and were teaching.

> The Christians of Pergamos were like the Christians of Corinth as Paul wrote to them in 1 Corinthians 5:1–9. They were too "tolerant" of false doctrines and immoral living, and Jesus had to rebuke them. Satan couldn't accomplish much by persecution, because many did hold fast, like Antipas. So Satan tried to accomplish his goals by using deception; first he used violence, then he used alliance. A difficult environment never justifies compromise. It is easy for a church in such difficulty to justify this compromise in the

name of "we need all the help we can get." But no church needs that kind of help.[83]

As mentioned briefly earlier, the Niciolaitans had developed a system of hierarchical dominance to conquer the people and bring them under oppression. They also practiced immoral behavior and illicit sexual activities with little or no adherence to godliness. When the mind and heart become corrupt and one justifies himself to gratify the flesh, he gives little attention to the rebuke of the Spirit. This is what was happening at Pergamos. Not only did they observe the actions of the Nicolaitans, but some also adopted the practice and established a doctrine. Remember that this practice developed from within the church. Nicolaus, one of the first deacons in the church who was a proselyte, fell into heresy and used his influence to corrupt others. It is believed that from him came the group called the Nicolaitans.

> There were some who taught that it was lawful to eat things sacrificed to idols, and that simple fornication was no sin; they, by an impure worship, drew men into impure practices, as Balaam did the Israelites. Observe, (1.) The filthiness of the spirit and the filthiness of the flesh often to together. Corrupt doctrines and corrupt worship often lead to a corrupt conversation. (2.) It is very lawful to fix the name of the leaders on any heresy upon those who follow them. It is the shortest way of telling who we mean. (3.) To continue in communion with persons of corrupt principles and practices is displeasing to God, draws guilt and blemish upon the whole society: they become partakers of others men's sins. Though the church, as church, has no power to punish the persons of men, either for heresy of immorality,

---

83 David Guzik. Rev. 2.

with corporal penalties, yet it has power to exclude them from its communion; and, if not so, Christ, the head and lawgiver of the church will be displeased with it.[84]

This is what the church today needs to be aware of: there are more false teachers today than there were in Pergamos, and the means of delivery is far greater than it was then. However, the desire to gratify the flesh has created a spiritual blindness in the church. This warrants the rebuke of Christ and the adherence of the church if it is to avoid leaving its first love and falling into apostasy. The call to the church of Pergamos by Christ was for their quick response to repentance, to think differently, reconsider, or he would come quickly and fight against them with the sword of his mouth.

Christ concludes this letter similarly to how he introduced himself. He is using the same two-edged sword, "his word" out of his mouth, as mentioned in the introduction, which cuts deeper than a weapon that can only hurt the flesh. He that hath an ear should hear what the Spirit says to the churches, not only to the churches then, but even more so now. Suffice it to say, there is a spiritual deafness in the church today. And the deafness begins with the leadership, which is the exact reason that Christ sent the letters to the leadership of the churches.

The greatest influence comes from the top. As the old saying goes, you can't cleanse the stream from the middle. It must start where the flow of water begins and filters down. Many churches are established on the wrong foundation and with wrong motives and have a negative impact on the congregants. There is a promise to those who overcome, not to all who hear, to eat of "hidden manna," which suggests feeding. But what it will be is not known.

---

84   Clarence Larkin, 1128.

Those "that overcometh" (v. 17) will be given "hidden manna ... a stone, and ... a new name." The passage is nebulous; the interpretation may be clear to those in the Tribulation, but the "hidden manna" refers to the miraculous feeding of Israel in the wilderness detailed in Exodus 16:4–36 and the manna placed in the "pot" to be put in the ark of the covenant (Exodus 16:33). Manna is also identified with "bread from heaven" in John 6:31–33.[85]

He will give the overcomers a "white stone," which carries much symbolism. In ancient times, a white stone was given as a victory stone. It was sometimes given as evidence when pardon is offered. Judges would have both black and white stones in a criminal case, and he issued the stone according to his decision. If the judge gave a black stone, the criminal or convict would be condemned; if a white stone, the offender was pardoned and was free of consequence. "Conquerors in the public games were also given white stones with their names in them, which entitled them to be supported the rest of their lives at public expense."[86]

It is possible that Christ had all three purposes in mind when he promised the overcomers a white stone, which they would be acquainted with. Jesus did say that on the white stone the new name would be written. This new name was also promised to the Gentiles who received the adoption as sons. "And the Gentiles shall see thy righteousness, and all kings thy glory: and thou shalt be called by a new name, which the mouth of the Lord shall name" (Isaiah 62:2). The new name would be known only by those who received it.

---

85 George Grace, 34.
86 Finis Dake, 287, i.

CHAPTER 7

The Church of Thyatira

The fourth letter was sent to the church of Thyatira. Thyatira was located southeast of Pergamum and slightly northwest of Sardis and was approximately thirty miles from the Aegean coastline. It was in a small city that became well known for its manufacturing. Today, the city of Akhisar is located there.

Thyatira is mentioned only four times in the Bible, three in Revelation 1–2 and once in Acts 16 where the apostles went to Macedonia on their missionary journey and came to Philippi as led by the Spirit. They came to a place of prayer to speak to the women who were gathered. "And a certain woman named Lydia, a seller of purple, of the city of Thyatira, which worshipped God, heard us: whose heart the Lord opened, that she attended unto the things which were spoken of Paul" (Acts 16:14). This was not one of the most famous cities and was among the smallest of them, strategically located between Lydia and Mysia.

Because of its location in the center of the large level plain, the city had few natural defenses. Archaeological evidence demonstrates that a settlement existed here as early as 3000 B.C.E. During the 5th century B.C.E., the Persians gained control of the area, followed by Alexander the Great toward the 4th century. At the beginning of the 3rd century, the Seleucid ruler Seleucus I Nicator re-founded the city and apparently settled Macedonian soldiers in the city. Serving as a military outpost. Thyatira became a part of the Pergamene kingdom under the Attalid rulers by 189 B.C.E. (if not earlier). After Attalus III bequeathed his Pergamene kingdom to the Romans in 133 B.C.E., the Romans established the province of Asia in 129 B.C.E. and Thyatira came under Roman rule. Located at the crossroads of the major route leading northwest to Pergamum, southeast to Sardis, and southwest to Magnesia and Smyrna. Thyatira became an important trade, industrial, and commercial center. Inscriptional evidence indicates that the city was host to numerous trade guilds, which functioned as a social, civic, and religious clubs or organizations.[87]

Thyatira may have been the smallest of the cities, but it received the largest of the letters sent by Christ, which will be seen later.

As noted in Acts, Lydia converted and was baptized, she and her household, and entreated Paul and Silas to lodge within her house on their visit to the area. Obviously, she was not among the poor based on her profession, as she was a seller of purple, a color often worn by kings and nobles. "Thyatira was in a rich agricultural area and was a city of commerce, including wool and linen workers, garment makers, leather workers, potters and bronze smiths. It was famous

---

[87] Clyde E. Fant, and Mitchell G. Reddish, 328.

for the making of purple dye, the color of the raiment of kings and dignitaries."[88]

It is not known exactly by whom the church was established in Thyatira. Some believe it may have been established by the apostle Paul's associate, or even by Lydia, who may have had great influence, as she was indigenous of Thyatira. Like most of the surrounding areas, there were ancient religious affinities, as there were temples in Thyatira that were dedicated to Apollo, the sun god. "Historically, the Thyatira period takes us from 500 A.D. to approximately 1000–1200 A.D. This church not only left its first love, but its first 'works' (v. 19)! This church had not only parted from Christ inwardly, but also outwardly."[89]

Not much is said of this church in terms of its suffering for Christ or its persecution, but it certainly was among the mix of churches that received a letter from the Lord via John the divine. This church, whose name means "odor of affliction," is also considered to be the apostate church, and although it is commended for faith, it is rebuked for its tolerance of Jezebel.

The Letter to Thyatira

As indicated previously, the longest of the letters Jesus sent was to the church of Thyatira, which is considered the smallest of the cities. Like the other letters and churches, attention must be paid to Christ's introduction of himself. The address to the angel had already been noted from the previous churches. However, Christ's introduction of himself is paramount and critical for each church. "These things saith the Son of God, who hath his eyes like unto a flame of fire, and

---

[88] White Wing Publishing House, *The Seven Churches of Asia*. "Know your Bible Series" (White Wing Publishing House and Press, Cleveland, Tennessee, 2002), 73.

[89] George Grace, 36.

his feet like fine brass." This powerful introduction is an attention-getter, as "these things saith the Son of God" opens the door to his divine nature.

> Jesus first describes Himself with a title that emphasizes His deity. In Jewish thought, to be the son of a thing meant you had the nature of that thing. The sons of the sorceress (Isaiah 57:3) had the nature of the sorceress. The sons of thunder (Mark 3:17) had the nature like thunder. So the Son of God has the divine nature, the nature of God.[90]

His penetrating, all-seeing eyes speak of his omniscience. His feet, which are pure brass, speaks of judgment and may suggest that he who knows every act and intention of the heart will judge with justice and due recompense. "I know thy works and charity."(Revelation 2:9) This is a church that has been complimented for its charity; benevolence; love-feast (*ag-ah-pay*), as it exercised unending love; service (*dee-ak-on-ee-ah*), especially of the Christian teacher, minister, or of the diaconate, as the servants of this church had done an amazing job. They had great faith (*pis-tis*), persuasion, moral conviction, and reliance upon Christ. They also were patient in their ability to continue to serve, enduring challenges, although Thyatira was not known as a persecuted church.

However, everyone who is called in the name of Christ will suffer persecution designed and executed by the Devil. Here, Christ mentioned their works a second time and noted that, this time, it is more than the first. They had an extensive record of works; however, it is important to have more than works and service because Christ sees everything. In other words, works and service are great, but faithfulness in all aspects of a Christian's life is more important. Christ,

---

90 David Guzik

the just judge with eyes of flaming fire, sees every detail of what one does, and he made that quite clear here.

However, he had a few things against them. The first thing was their allowing Jezebel to teach in the church. Churches would be advised to vet carefully who they allow to teach in Christ's church. The expression Jesus used about this woman is one of disdain: "Thou sufferest that woman Jezebel, which calleth herself a prophetess, to teach and to seduce my servants to commit fornication and to eat things offered unto idols" (v. 20). There are many different thoughts concerning the use of the name Jezebel. Clearly, this does not speak of an individual but rather a spirit or character.

Jezebel the Prophetess

This woman has been proven to be a false prophetess and an immoral character who seduced God's people into sinning. If she is referred to symbolically, compared to Jezebel in the Old Testament, she is indeed a deceiver and a manipulator, one who is conniving and should not be trusted or followed. There is a certain connotation attached to the name. She was naturally evil, as the Bible says that the Devil is the author of evil.

Jezebel in the Old Testament lied concerning Naboth and had him stoned to death in order to make it possible for her husband, Ahab, to get Naboth's piece of land given to him as his heritage (1 Kings 21). She threatened Elijah the prophet after he destroyed all the prophets of Baal. She was the first woman to paint her face in her attempt to disguise herself from God and the prophets. She was the woman about whom God told Elijah that dogs would eat her flesh and lick Ahab's blood in the same place where dogs licked Naboth's blood in Samaria. So if this woman mentioned in Thyatira is symbolic or similar in character to Jezebel of the Old Testament, it is not surprising what she had been able to do within the church with those who were vulnerable.

> This false teacher is referred to as "Jezebel," which may or may not have actually been her name, but certainly refers to her spirit. It references Jezebel in the Old Testament, who was the wife of King Ahab. She was an idolatrous woman with unscrupulous methods, to perpetuate her power. Jesus warned the church of Thyatira of coming judgment to this false teacher and all those who commit spiritual adultery by moral compromise. This "Jezebel" was given time to repent, but refused. (Rev. 2 v. 21).[91]

Paul talked to the elders about watching for spiritual predators whose interest was their own personal gratification. While a church is in danger of false teaching creeping into its congregation at all times, it is most susceptible when it develops from within. Tolerance and compromise are two different things. While some of these saints were able to tolerate this Jezebel, maybe because of hierarchical position, they did not compromise the doctrines of good Christian living that they had been taught. They were able to not become "partakers of other men's sins," or woman for that matter. At the same time, there were others who did not have the same level of endurance and fortitude to resist Jezebel's influence.

The churches today are not in a much better position than the church of Thyatira because there are many false prophets and prophetesses today who must be guarded against or they will create major damage to the church. As a matter of fact, many lives have been disrupted with false teachers, false apostles, and false prophets. There

---

91 Discover the Book of Revelation, http://www.discoverrevelation.com/Rev_2.html. (accessed September 5, 2013).

is a great influx of so-called prophets and prophetesses who do not even have a good understanding of God's Word and are pretending to have a "word from the Lord" for churches. And many are causing havoc like tornadoes as they move across churches.

> The major problem at Thyatira was the church's toleration of a woman symbolically called Jezebel. This woman, considered a false prophet and teacher, was a seducer who led the people astray, causing them to "eat things food sacrificed to idols" and to "commit adultery with her" (2:20, 22). (Jezebel, an infamous character from the Hebrew Bible, was the wife of King Ahab of Israel. She was a promoter of Baal worship and a persecutor of the prophets of the God of Israel.) The accusation that the Jezebel of Thyatira caused people to "commit adultery with her" is a metaphor for her leading them to be unfaithful to God. The specific way she led them astray was her acceptance and perhaps even encouragement of Christians eating meat that had been ritually offered to other gods, as much of the meat sold in the markets of the ancient world had been.[92]

There is another thought that suggests that this might have been a real woman who actually married someone from the church that gave her significant access and privilege to minister in the church. It is believed that she had an affiliation with a guild that practices sexual immorality. The idea, however, that this is a real woman could be hard to prove, but here is what one author writes concerning Jezebel of Thyatira:

> History intimates that "that woman Jezebel" was a business woman, and probably involved in the guild ties mentioned

---

92   Clyde E Fant, and Mitchell G Redding, 330.

> earlier. It is conjectured that this marriage, too, might have been with an eye for more congenial commercial relations between the Christian and pagan elements of Thyatira. Again from history, some manuscripts give reason to think that "Jezebel" was the pastor's wife. This line of thinking was been offered as the reason for the woman having such preponderance of influence in the church—that she had her pastor-husband's blessing in what she was doing, and that she took advantage of this favor to usurp authority as Jezebel of old had done—to wield an ever-widening control in church matters.[93]

Whatever or whoever Jezebel was, she was a major factor that caused the corruption of the church in Thyatira. Churches must guard against every heretical teaching and immoral behavior, but nothing is more important to guard against than sexual immorality. Christians ought to avoid joining themselves to harlotry and fornication. While one might say that all sin is sin, there are some that will impact your life forever and also do greater damage to you and the reputation of the kingdom of God.

> What? Know ye not that he which is joined to an harlot is one body? For two, saith he, shall be one flesh. But he that is joined unto the Lord is one spirit. Flee fornication. Every sin that a man doeth is without the body; but he that committeth fornication sinneth against his own body. (1 Corinthians 6:16–18)

Any form of adultery, fornication, or idolatry is an offense to God, and because he is jealous, he will take offensive action. Christ said

---

[93] White Wing Publishing, 78.

he gave Jezebel space to repent, but she did not. Christ, who is full of mercy, always gives the sinner a chance to make amends, and only when the opportunity for repentance is ruined will God apply the consequences.

> The woman herself knew exactly when her "space to repent" had been offered. She had let it pass because the cost seemed too great—the loss of her elevated posture, her prestige as a "prophetess." To repent would have meant an open confession, the asking for forgiveness, and the proving of herself in the eyes and minds of the church, as well as those she had led astray. But now, surely they would all recognize her, even if her name was not really Jezebel. Unless her followers believed in her more than in the message of the letter, her days were numbered.[94]

As a result of Jezebel's non-repentance, God decided to cast her into a "bed," or *klee-nay*, which suggests a cough or sickness, and those with her into great tribulation, or *thlip-sis*, which means pressure, literally or figuratively, to be afflicted; to be in anguish; to be burdened, and to have trouble, except there is repentance of such deeds.[95]

Clarence Larkin has another twist as to who Jezebel might have been in his book on Revelation.

> Who this woman was is in a question. She was a "pretender," and called herself a "prophetess." Probably she was of noble lineage. She certainly was a woman of commanding influence. Whether her real name was Jezebel or not, she was so like

---

[94] White Wing Publishing, 83.
[95] Brian Thomas Webb, Strong's Concordance for iPhone version 1.5.3, Copyright 2009.

her prototype in the Old Testament, Jezebel the wife of Ahab, that Christ called her by that name.[96]

The next step Jesus planned to take was to kill Jezebel's children. "I will kill her children with death" is a drastic statement, which may speak of total destruction and separation from God. It is believed by some that this thought referenced as far as the second death, which is total separation from God. But whatever the interpretation, one can only conclude that the consequences will be severe. The reason for this severe promise of judgment is so others will learn.

Paul told Timothy, "Them that sin rebuke before all, that others also may fear" (1 Timothy 5:20). Christ promised to make an example out of Jezebel and her affiliates and partners in crime so all the other churches would know that he searches each man's heart and will execute recompense for works done as he sees fit. It is important to note Christ's promise to those who were not partakers of Jezebel's sins. He promised the rest of the church of Thyatira—all who had not involved themselves with Jezebel, did not believe and accept her doctrine, and did not know the depths of Satan—that he would put no further burden on them. However, they were to hold fast to what they had till he came, for drifting from it would be to their detriment.

Christ's introduction of himself to this church as the one whose eye is as a flame of fire was proving his knowledge of all who had not gotten involved. God's promise to Abraham was that he would not destroy the righteous with the wicked. Many of the saints at Thyatira were faithful and were admonished, "Hold fast till I come." His reward would be to pay every man according to his works.

> There were many faithful, uncompromising Christians in Thyatira. To them, Jesus simply says hold fast! They must not

---

[96] Clarence Larkin, 24.

stop doing what is good. They must not become distracted of discouraged for what Jesus wants them to be and to do ... Even when there is the immoral and idolatrous influence of a Jezebel, Christians can overcome and keep Jesus' works until the end. We must not become overly discouraged at immorality and idolatry around us, even among Christians. God's work will still go on through his overcomers ... Jesus promised that His people would reign with Him. Here, there is a special promise to those who overcome the threat of immorality and idolatry. To them, Jesus offers a share in His kingdom.[97]

He would also give them power over the nations to rule with a rod of iron. The symbolism of this rod of iron is twofold: it speaks of the baton of royalty, or a staff.

The significant difference is it is of iron, which suggests its strength and unbreakable quality. This means that the finding of guilt and the subsequent ruling cannot be broken or changed because it is done with a rod of iron. Therefore, it is final. This is an amazing promise to believers who overcome. They will sit with Christ on his throne when he will judge the nations, and as part of their reward for holding fast, they will be on the seat of judgment with Christ. "I will allow everyone who wins the victory to sit with me on my throne, as I have won the victory and have sat down with my Father on his throne" (Revelation 3:21 GWT).[98]

"They will be broken to 'Shivers'," or *soon-tree-bo,* which means to be crushed completely, to shatter. Two thoughts here. One, all those who were once rulers will find their authority crushed under the sole authority of Christ, his saints being with him. Two, there is

---

[97] David Guzik, Rev., 2.

[98] God's Word Translation, http://www.biblegateway.com/passage/?search=Revelation%203&version=GW. (accessed September 13, 2013).

no doubt that when the lost are told of their fate, they will be crushed as they face eternal separation from the Lord.

The overcomers are also promised "the morning star," which, by all accounts, will be Christ himself, as he mentions in Revelation 22, "I, Jesus, have sent mine angel to testify unto you these things in the churches, I am the root and the offspring of David, and the bright and morning star" (Revelation 22:16).

> Christ himself is "the bright and morning star" (Revelation 22:16). He will give the overcomers Himself, as it were. Just as the morning star in the heavens ushers in the glorious brightness of the new day, Christ is the herald of our eternity. With Him we will have "eternal day."[99]

Finally, to the church of Thyatira, like all the other churches, "He that hath an ear, let him hear what the Spirit saith unto the churches." Consequences will be removed and rewards will be given to all who hear and listen to the Holy Spirit of truth. The instructions of Christ, if ignored, carry unprecedented consequences.

---

99 White Wing Publishing, 83.

CHAPTER 8

THE CHURCH OF SARDIS

Sardis was located in the district of Lydia to the south, slightly east of Thyatira and northwest of Philadelphia. The fifth of Jesus' seven letters was sent to this church.

Sardis was the capital of Lydia and had a great history of wealth and fertility, but like most cities in ancient Asia Minor, it had problems with immorality and idol worship. By the time John was sent there, however, Sardis had already lost some of its great strength. Yet it still contains a significant portion of the largest third-century synagogues outside Palestine and remains a place with great history from ancient times, both from battles fought and Christian struggles. There is some uncertainty as to whether it had a name change tracing back to the fifth or sixth century as referenced in the Old Testament.

The earliest biblical reference to Sardis may occur in Obadiah 20. This text, written in the 6th of 5th century B.C.E.,

> proclaims the eventual return of Judah's exile to the promise land. The verse claims that "the exiles of Jerusalem who are in Sepharad shall possess the towns of the Negeb." The identity of Sepharad is unknown, but because of linguistic similarities between Sepharad and Sfard (the Lydian and Persian word for Sardis), the possibility that Sepharad is ancient Sardis is strong.[100]

Sardis, like many other places, have been through different changes and controlling powers. It lost its status as the capital of the Lydian kingdom under Croesus after being captured by Cyrus, king of Persia, whose reign lasted until the city surrendered to Alexander the Great. After Alexander's death, came the Seleucids.

> The city lay north-east of Ephesus on a spur of Mount Tmolus and its history went back some one thousand years before Christ. It was taken by Alexander in 334 BC and then under the Seleucid dynasty became an administrative center, which subsequently comprised the capital of Roman federation.[101]

During the time the Romans were ruling the city, it had great success and prospered, but because of its history of battles and conquests, this city often had to be renovated and its infrastructure rebuilt. Not only did it have to deal with destruction by man, but it also suffered major damage to buildings by earthquakes during the seventh century. "During the 8th century, Arabs attacked the city, and beginning in the 11th century, the city was intermittently under the control of Seljuk

---

100 Clyde E. Fant and Mitchell G. Reddish, 306.
101 Peter Lorie. Revelation, "St. John the Divine's Prophecies of the Apocalypse and Beyond" Labyrinth Publishing (UK) Ltd, 1994, 67.

Turks. Occupation of Sardis came to an end in 1402, when Mongol Turk Tamerlane (or Timur) sacked the city."[102]

For more than eleven hundred years, this city had seen an incredible number of changes in government and leadership, most of them taking over by force from one conquest to another. Not only did these changes result in political differences but also cultural and religious transitions. History shows that Sardis had a large population of Jews and Christians, but history also confirms that the religious differences were stark.

This small embattled city had to deal with the open differences of Judaism and Christianity but even more so with the rampant idolatry, adultery, and fornication as well as various deities. There were only a "few in Sardis," as Jesus stated in his letter, who had not defiled their garments.

> The patron deities of Sardis were Cybele and Artemis. Remains of the temple to Artemis are still standing. Both Judaism and Christianity also flourished in Sardis. According to the Jewish historian Josephus (37 C.E–100 C.E.), Antiochus III transported 2,000 loyal Jewish families from Mesopotamia and settled them in Phrygia and Lidia (Jewish Antiquities 12. 147-153) … Josephus reports also that the Roman emperor Augustus gave orders that the Jews of Sardis were not to be prevented from collecting funds (apparently the half-shekel temple tax) to be sent to Jerusalem (Jewish Antiquities 16. 171). The presence of a prominent, large synagogue, in use as early as the 3rd century C.E., gives solid testimony to the sizeable population of Jews in Sardis and their social importance. Christianity had taken root in the city by the end of the first century, as evidenced by its mention in the

---

102 Clyde E. Fant and Mitchell G. Reddish, 305.

book of Revelation (1:11; 3:1–6). During the 2nd century the bishop of Sardis, Melito, was an outspoken church leader who was involved in the Quartodeciman controversy (concerning the correct date on which to celebrate Easter). Sardis continued to be the seat of an important bishopric until the 14th century. During this time several churches were build at Sardis; some of their remains are still visible.[103]

Sardis earned the reputation as the chief city of Asia Minor. It is one of the most ancient of the cities, and the first among the cities to manufacture gold and silver coins during the days of Croesus. With this great history of wealth, treasure, and development, it can be understood why so many of the rulers around would have wanted to get their hands on this city. This was a city rich with commerce with its vast manufacturers of textile, dyes, jewelry, and much more. Its wealth became its worst enemy because of its covetous neighboring countries, much like some of today's oil-rich countries that others want to get their hands on.

Great treasure generates great attention, and that was one of the many downfalls of Sardis, and it was often taken by force. However, one should always remember that a more wicked man will always get the edge over another wicked man. Jesus told Peter, "Put up again thy sword into its place: for all they that take the sword shall perish with the sword" (Matthew 26:52).

> One writer, without elaboration, dates the founding of Sardis as 1200 B.C. In about 556 B.C., Croesus, king of Lydia, ushered in "the Golden Age of Sardis" from wealth gathered from gold mines and trade. But King Cyrus of Persia took the city in 546 B.C., and he is said to have taken $600,000,000 worth

---

103 Clyde E. Fant and Mitchell G. Reddish, 305.

> of treasure. In 344 B.C. Sardis surrendered to Alexander the Great, but was taken by Antiochus the great in 214 B.C. He in turn was defeated by the Romans in 190 B.C., and it was under the Roman rule when the church received the letter on record in Revelation 3:1–6.[104]

This church was called the dead church, although its name means that it lives. In the midst of its struggles and failures, like every time and church period throughout history, God has never been left without a remnant holding the banner of victory and keeping themselves unspotted from the world.

> In the panorama of church history, Sardis represents the Protestant church during the, period between A.D.1517 and approximately A.D. 1800. It began, I believe, when Martin Luther nailed his Ninety-Five Theses on the chapel door of the church at Wittenberg, Germany. It is an era which started with the Reformation and takes us into the beginning of the great missionary movement in the history of the church.[105]

The Letter to Sardis

The letter is again sent to the angel of the church as it was with all the others. The man in charge, the man at the helm, has the voice to proclaim what is written. The letter is sent to the strong man of the house to declare what thus saith the Lord. Thus Jesus introduced himself to Sardis uniquely and exclusively. No other church was like Sardis in general, although they almost all had faults mingled with faithfulness.

---

104 White Wing Publishing, 88.
105 Vernon G. McGee, 29.

"These things saith he that hath the seven Spirits of God." (Revelation 3:1) There are a couple of things to look at when observing this statement. The reference of seven is more symbolic to completion, totality, and perfection than it is in reference to numbers. Another thing to look at is the word *Spirit* as it is used here.

The word is *pneu-mah*, a current of air, breath, as it pertains to humans, it speaks of "the rational soul," the "vital principle", and mental disposition: From a superhuman standpoint, it speaks of an angel, the divine God, and life.[106] This might be a lot to absorb, but it gives a little perspective on the broad use of the word *spirit*. Christ is describing himself as the ultimate authority and master of all spirits, evil or good, seen or unseen. Everything is perfected and complete in him.

Let's go back to what the apostle Paul said to the saints at Corinth: "But God hath revealed them unto us by his Spirit: for the Spirit searcheth all things, yeah, the deep things of God" (1 Corinthians 2:9). It is through the Spirit that all things are communicated between God/Christ and man, and an understanding of the fullness of the Spirit in Christ will let the church know ultimately that everything is open before Christ.

In Christ dwells the fullness of the Godhead, so he has the fullness of the Spirit. And not only so, he also has the fullness of the church, which is his body, by having full authority over the leaders of the church. As stated clearly in Revelation 1:20, "The mystery of the 'seven stars' which thou sawest in my right hand, and the seven golden candlesticks. The seven stars are the angels of the churches: and the seven candlesticks which thou sawest are the seven churches."

It cannot be overstated that the level of authority, domination, intimidation, and, likewise, the feeling of trepidation the angel (pastor/

---

106 Brian Thomas Webb, Strong's Concordance for iPhone version 1.5.3, Copyright 2009.

leader) of the church must have felt was tremendous when hearing Christ say in technical terms, "You are in my hands," referring to the vessel of the potter who, in his hand, cannot say to the potter, "Do not break or make me in that form." This sets the stage for the remaining portion of the letter: "I know thy works!"

This church had a name, *on-om-ah*, which speaks of authority and character. In other words, this church had been known to be alive. It had a name that thou livest, *dzah-o,* which means literally or figuratively to be quick, or full of life.

The problem seemed to be at that time was that all the church had was the name, as the character was no longer there. It had the name of life, but was a dead, or *nek-ros,* corpse. This church was only the corpse of what it was known to be, a bare skeleton of itself. David Guzik has a heart-wrenching thought on this subject, as noted along with a couple of his admired commentators below:

But you are dead.

    a. Dead: Despite their reputation of life, Jesus saw them for what they really were. But you are dead shows that a good reputation is no guarantee of true spiritual character. Despite their good appearance, Jesus saw them for what they really were.

    b. Dead indicates no struggle, Jesus saw no fight, no persecution. It wasn't that the church at Sardis was losing the battle. A dead body has lost the battle, and the fight seems over. In this letter, Jesus doesn't encourage the Christians in Sardis to stand strong against persecution or false doctrine, probably because there simply wasn't a significant danger of these things in Sardis. Being dead, the church in Sardis presented no significant threat to Satan's domain, so it wasn't worth attacking.

    c. The church in Sardis was "a perfect model of inoffensive Christianity" (Caird). Another commentator says, "It was not scandalous wickedness, but decent death; the form retained, the heart gone."

    d. "The church of Sardis was at peace—but it was the peace of the dead." (Barclay).[107]

What Jesus had against this church was it allowed itself to go dead. It had succumbed to external pressure and activities that drained it of its spiritual life. This church had seen unthinkable decay. A church that is dead has lost all its vital functions. In a body that is dead all its organs are also dead. Therefore, in a dead church, worship becomes nothing more than an act; zeal is weakened as is fellowship; the manifestation of the Spirit is absent; communion with God and each other is, at best, on a downward spiral, and nothing remains with which to resist the wiles of the Devil or quench his fiery darts. It has given up fighting. It does not have a pulse!

> The church of Sardis was called a "Dead Church" though it had a name to live. That is, it was a "Formalistic Church," a church given over to "formal" or "ritualistic" worship. It had the "Form of Godliness without the power." The meaning of "Sardis" is the "escaping one," or those who "come out" and so it is an excellent type of the Church of the Reformation Period.[108]

---

107 David Guzik, Rev., 2.
108 Clarence Larkin, 25.

There is always the danger of wearing a façade, which was the experience of the church of Sardis. From the outside it was known to have life; it had a name that it was alive. This suggested at least a couple of things. One, it was living in the shadow of its past, hiding under the umbrella of what was. And two, its name was nothing but a name. There was never the character and lifestyle that goes along with it.

There are many churches today that have the same characteristics. From the outside, they look good, do a lot of community work, feed the poor, and shelter the homeless. As a result, they carry the good name of a great church in the community. However, they lack the power and anointing of the Holy Spirit. They cause the community to live, but they do not offer real life. The apostle Paul warned Timothy that in the last days it would get to this point.

> For men shall be lovers of their own selves, covetous, boasters, proud, blasphemers, disobedient to parents, unthankful, unholy, Without natural affection, trucebreakers, false accusers, incontinent, fierce, despisers of those that are good, Traitors, heady, highminded, lovers of pleasures more than lovers of God; Having a form of godliness, but denying the power thereof: from such turn away. For of this sort are they which creep into houses, and lead captive silly women with sins, led away with divers lusts, Ever learning, and never able to come to the knowledge of the truth. (2 Timothy 3:2–7)

Jesus rebuked the scribes, Pharisees, and hypocrites who looked one way outwardly but was completely different inwardly. "Woe to you, scribes and Pharisees, hypocrites! For you are like whitewashed tombs, which outwardly appear beautiful, but within are full of dead people's bones and pall uncleanness"(Matthew 23:27 ESV).[109] To pretend to be something that one is not is never acceptable to the Lord. Be "watchful." This word is *gray-gor-yoo-o,* and it means to keep awake, i.e., to watch, to be vigilant and watchful.[110]

Apparently, in the eyes of Christ, this church had fallen asleep spiritually, which caused its dead state. However, there was some sign of life that needed immediate attention. The call was to strengthen the remnant who was on the verge of dying. Christ had not given up on them. The situation was grave but not hopeless. In Martha's conversation with Jesus in John 11, she said unto him, "Lord, if thou hast been here, my brother had not died." Jesus told her that her brother would live again.

Martha thought that this would only be possible in the resurrection on the last day, especially since Lazarus had been dead for three days. However, it was made clear when Jesus declared, "I am the resurrection, and the life: he that believeth in me, though he were dead, yet shall he live" (John 11:25). The same scenario seems to have been playing out at Sardis, as they were dead but there was hope.

Watchfulness is one key element in the life and spirituality of the church. If a church or an individual is not watchful, the Devil will cause mass destruction, as he is everywhere, seeking who he may devour. To be off watch is to give access to the Enemy, and he comes only to "steal, kill, and destroy." The Imperfection of this church was notable upon Jesus' assessment. "For I have not found thy work perfect before God," he said. Their works were not complete. They were underperforming as the result of not watching. Matthew Henry says that they were

---

109 English Standard Version, http://www.biblegateway.com/passage/?search=Matthew%2023&version=ESV. (accessed September 13, 2013).

110 Brian Thomas Webb.

> Not filled up; there is something wanting in them; there is the shell, but not the kernel; there is the carcase, but not the soul—the shadow, but not the substance. The inward thing is wanting, thy works are hollow and empty; prayers are not filled up with holy desires, alms-deeds not filled up with true charity, sabbaths not filled up with suitable devotion of soul to God; there are not inward affections suitable to outward acts and expressions. Now when the spirit is wanting the form cannot long subsist. To recollect themselves, and remember how they have received and heard (v. 3); what messages they had received from God, what tokens of his mercy and favor towards them, what sermons they had heard, but how they had received and heard, what impressions the mercies of God had made upon their souls at first, what affections they felt working under the word and ordinances, the love of their espousals, the kindness of their youth, how welcome the gospel and the grace of God were to them when they first receive them.[111]

What seems to have happened to this church was that they had forgotten, or failed to adhere to the teaching of which they once held fast. This is typical to what Paul told Timothy concerning the constant preaching of the word in season and out. "For the time will come when they will not endure sound doctrine; but after their own lusts shall they heap to themselves teachers, having itching ears; and shall turn away their ears from the truth, and shall be turned unto fables" (2 Timothy 4:3–4).

It is hard not to compare the church of Ephesus with the church of Sardis because they were in somewhat similar positions. They both were enthusiastic at the starting point, but they faltered dramatically

---

[111] Matthew Henry, 1131.

in the end. It is clear, however, that Sardis was dealt a more serious blow than Ephesus. Ephesus left its first love and went cold; Sardis had the name that it was alive, but was dead. Both were instructed to remember. Ephesus was to remember from when it had fallen, repent and do its first work, or face severe consequences. Sardis was told to remember how it had received and heard, and hold fast, and repent or, likewise, face the consequences.

The truth is that corrections cannot be made without acknowledgment of the wrong; one will not make the effort to find the right path if one is not conscious that one is lost or going in the wrong direction. The prodigal son mentioned in Luke 15 kept drifting and going further into degradation until he "came to himself" and remembered home. The Scripture made it clear that he had done nothing to make correction until he came to himself at his lowest point. This church at its lowest point, when most of the congregation had already died, needed to be resuscitated with four-hundred volts of quickening Spirit so they could all begin to breathe again, as Ezekiel prophesied to the dry bones in the valley (Ezekiel 37).

> Living in the midst of a grossly secular society, where immorality knows no restraint and integrity is only a word, temptation to compromise God's Word of truth is strong … Early pangs of conscience are soon quieted, and self-justification pleads "wisdom," "freedom," and "no harm." Spiritual death comes slowly. Like the frog that was put in cool water which was heated gradually to the boiling point, bringing its death without resistance—numbly and without suffering—even so one compromise after another soon result in SIN, but under "pretty names." "And the wages of

sin is DEATH" (Romans 6:23), alike to the unbeliever and the backslidden Christian or church member.[112]

God has promised forgiveness for every wrong, iniquity, sin, and transgression. However, nothing is automatically forgiven, only when they are truly repented of. That's why Christ's instruction to the church is to repent, which means to be sorry but also to turn from.

The threat was that Christ would come on them "as a thief." This reference is not speaking of his second advent to the earth but rather of his coming in judgment to an unrepentant church. It also suggests that there will not be another message of warning following this one; the next would be the reward or penalty for not taking heed to the letter. There would not be a day that they could expect him to come in judgment. Rather, every day they should expect his return to Sardis.

> The advice which he gives to the Sardians is, in a way, universally suitable to human nature: "Be watchful; be more careful; carry out more completely and thoroughly what you have still to do, for hitherto you have always erred in leaving work half done and incomplete. Try to make that eager attention with which you at the beginning listened to the Gospel, and the enthusiasm with which at first you accepted it, a permanent feature in your conduct. If you are not watchful, you will not be ready at the moment of need: my arrival will find you unprepared, because in an hour that ye think 'not the Son of Man cometh'; any one can make ready for a fixed hour, but you must be always ready for an unexpected hour."[113]

---

112 White Wing Publishing, 97.

113 William Mitchell Ramsay. (2011-11-09). *The Letters to the Seven Churches of Asia and Their Place in the Plan of the Apocalypse* (With Active Table of Contents) (Kindle Locations 4951-4953). . Kindle Edition.

Few Have Not Defiled Their Garments

As mentioned earlier, it doesn't matter what kind of natural disaster, dispensation, circumstances, or apostate situation, God will always have a remnant to carry the torch and fight the battles. While the number of saints are not known, calculating and determining that there were only a few who had not defiled their garments gives the picture that the greater portion were among the dead. It can be imagined how desperate it became for that church, knowing that Christ, who introduced himself as "the one who have the seven Spirits and seven stars in his hand," knew who were alive, who were dead, and those who were ready to die.

The dying of a church often takes time and gives room for repentance and reconciliation. One of the most painful things one can experience is to watch those around him die and not be able to help. Looking back at what Jesus said about this church, they had a name that they lived but were dead. They were told that they should repent and "strengthen the things that remained and were ready to die." (Revelation 3:2)

That is a profound and scary thought that even what was left of them were ready to die. Yet, in all of this, a few had enough resistance to evil that they kept themselves unspotted from the world. "Even among the dead Christians in Sardis, there is a faithful remnant. But there were only a few names. In Pergamos (Revelation 2:14) and in Thyatira (Revelation 2:20) there were a few bad among the good. But in Sardis there are a few good among the bad."[114]

This is really an interesting thought. There were few who were causing havoc in the two churches mentioned, Pergamos and Thyatira. Although these churches had only a few, they were really bad weeds and negative influences that destroyed the spirituality and adherence

---

114 David Guzik, Rev., 3.

to the doctrines. But to the credit to those few in Sardis, they lived among the dead but kept their garments undefiled.

Clarence Larkin, in his comparative theory and theology, suggests that the church of Sardis represents the "Reformation Period" in that it was able to push the circulation of the Scriptures but faced great sectarian opposition, and in their effort to spread and preserve the doctrine of "Justification by Faith," they suffered the consequences.

> While the reformers swept away much ritualistic and doctrinal rubbish they failed to recover the promise of the Second Advent. They turned to God from idols, but not to "wait for His Son from the heavens." The "Sardis Period" extended form A.D. 1520 to about A.D. 1750.[115]

There were a "few names" in Sardis that had not defiled their garments, a few who in the midst of spiritual suicide, or spiritual euthanasia, kept their garments from soil. There were a few who remained faithful to the Lord. They had not polluted their souls, tarnished their reputation, compromised their sanctity, or succumbed to internal or external pressures. As a result of their faithfulness, God promised them that they would walk with him in "white," signifying continued purity and holiness "for they are worthy, (*ax`-ee-os*, deserving; it is also a symbol of praise, and suggest the receiving of a due reward)[116] He that overcomes shall also be clothed in white raiment." (Revelation 3:4-5)

Something worthy of note here is the promise of restoration to those who have defiled their garments. It goes back to the previous verses where they were instructed to remember the words they had received and heard and to hold fast and repent. So redemption and restoration was promised to those who were defiled.

---

115 Clarence Larkin, 25.
116 James Strong, Strong Exhaustive Concordance, Greek Reference #514.

This is, of course, the very nature and character of God to not hold one hostage to his past if he repents. Repentance warrants justification, justification leads to sanctification, and sanctification leads to pureness/holiness. Hence, Christ's promise is that not only would those who had not defiled their garments be in white, but also those who repented and overcame. The following statement supports this thought: "And I will not blot out his name out of the book of life." (Revelation 3:5)

This is both a threat and a promise. Those who defiled their garments deserved for their names to be blotted out of the Book of Life, but obedience, repentance, and continuance would prevent elimination from it. This thought might be hard for some to grasp, but Finis Dake puts it well in his commentary on this verse, as follows:

> Here Christ promises not to blot the name out of the book of life of any man who will obey the commands of note e, above. What if some should refuse to obey these commands, would their names not be blotted out? If we say such is impossible we accuse God of using vain threats on his people. He definitely promised Moses concerning any man who sinned, HIM WILL I BLOT OUT OF MY BOOK (Ex. 32:32–33). The Psalmist by the Holy Ghost prayed that God would blot out the names of Judas and all like him (Psalm 69:25–28 with Acts 1:20). In Rev. 22:18–19 Christ again threatens to take the names of men out of the book of life if they take anything away from the words of the book of prophecy.[117]

There are many who will have different ideas concerning what Jesus says about blotting names out of the Book of Life. But to be exegetical

---

117 Finis Dake, Dake Annotated Reference Bible, Rev. 3, Note j.

of Scripture is not to believe when it ties into one's theory or doctrinal persuasion but rather to take it as the author intends and adjusts to meet its standard. The thought above is shared by David Guzik to certain extent when he says,

> There is a book of life, and there are five different references to people being blotted out of the Book of Life. This means that the idea of being blotted out of the Book of Life should be taken seriously. Perhaps it is only a symbol, and that persons names was never there to begin with. Even if that is the case, the Lord still wants us to take it seriously, because there are some who by every human appearance are saved, yet will not be in heaven.[118]

Whichever way one looks at this, one must remember that God does not say what he does not mean and has preordained. He requires of man that his yea be yea, and his nay, nay. He will not require of man more than he requires of himself.

The eyes of God are in every place, beholding the evil and the good, and will reward every man according to his work. Faithfulness and steadfastness are two of God's specialties. He greatly rewards faithfulness; those who endure to the end will have their reward. Those who die for their faith and are steadfast in not denying His name will be rewarded beyond human comprehension.

> But as it is written, eye hath not seen, nor ear heard, neither have entered into the heart of man, the things which God hath prepared for them that love him. But God hath revealed them unto us by his Spirit: for the Spirit searcheth all things, yea, the deep things of God. (1 Corinthians 2:9–10)

---

118 David Guzik, Rev., 3.

Christ promised not to blot out the names of the overcomers to his Father in heaven, but he will not leave it there. He will take it further by personally confessing them before the his Father.

The word *confess* is "*ex-om-ol-ogeh'-o*, which basically means to acknowledge, to agree fully, to profess, or to promise."[119] Jesus will first present the saints to himself and to his Father. This will be an extraordinary moment for Christ to finally present to the Father the ultimate fruit of his finished work. He will proudly stand before his Father and acknowledge those who have come through many battles and have persevered to the end, some unto death. By this time, one would imagine that many names will be blotted out of the book because they had not harkened unto the instructions given for restoration.

> But the names of those that overcome shall never be blotted out. Christ will produce this book of life, and confess the names of the faithful who stand there, before God, and all the angels; he will do this as their Judge, when the books shall be opened; he will do this as their captain and head, leading them with him triumphantly to heaven, presenting them to the Father: Behold me, and the children that thou hast given me. How great will this honour and reward me![120]

To say that it will be an interesting time when Christ confesses his saints before his Father and the angels is a gross understatement. It will be an overwhelming time and a moment of splendor for angels to behold. Just imagine what it will be like. Knowing that at the repentance of a sinner angels rejoice, one can only imagine what it will be like when they see the ransomed come home. "I say unto you, that likewise joy shall be in heaven over one sinner that repenteth, more

---

119 Brian Thomas Webb, Strong's Concordance for iPhone version 1.5.3, Copyright 2009.
120 Matthew Henry, 1133.

than over ninety and nine just persons, which need no repentance" (Luke 15:7).

The church of Sardis may have gotten caught up in the wealth and fame of its great city and lost focus on the doctrines of life. That danger is seen today in many churches and places where wealth and fame take precedence over righteous living. They appear to be alive but are dead. Much more will be said about this when looking at the church of Laodicea.

"He that hath an ear, let him hear what the Spirit saith to the churches."(Revelation 3:6) Saul faced severe consequences when he failed to do what he was instructed to by Samuel, who was God's messenger. In the end, he wanted to make sacrifice in an effort to make up for his disobedience, but Samuel had a surprising rebuke for him: "**Hath the** LORD *as great* delight in burnt offerings and sacrifices, as in obeying the voice of the LORD? Behold, to obey *is* better than sacrifice, *and* to hearken than the fat of rams" (1 Samuel 15:22). It would serve everyone well to listen and follow the Spirit when he speaks, not wait until after the allotted time given to try to move God to help.

CHAPTER 9

THE CHURCH OF PHILADELPHIA

Philadelphia is the sixth of the seven churches mentioned in Revelation for which John received a letter from Christ and was told to deliver it. Philadelphia, like most of the other churches, was located west in Asia Minor. It was located approximately thirty miles southeast of Sardis and directly north of Laodicea. Although Philadelphia had its own history, it is primarily remembered as one of the seven cities mentioned in Revelation where the church received a letter by the hand of John. The city was also located in an earthquake-prone area.

> The city was named for Attalus II Philadelphus, the Attalid king of Pergamum from 159 to 138 B.C.E., whose loyalty to his brother Eumenes II Soter, who preceeded him as king (r.197–159 B.C.E), earned him the nickname "Philadelphus,"

> meaning "brotherly love." Either Eumenes or Attalus founded the city, which was in the Lydian region of ancient Anatolia.[121]

Roman domination did not spare Philadelphia although it may not have been taken over by force. Around 133 BC, Philadelphia was left to the Romans by Attalus III.

> As cities went, it was not very ancient, for it had been founded by Attalus the Second in 140 B.C. Attalus was called Philadelphus, and it was after him that Philadelphia had been named. Although Philadelphia as a city was not very ancient, from the earliest times there had always been some kind of settlement on the site where it stood. It was one of the most strategic sites in the world. Philadelphia stood at the place where the borders of three countries—Mysia, Lydia, and Phrygia—met. It was strategically a border town.[122]

Because of its strategic location and position, Philadelphia was viewed as a gateway to the east of Asia Minor. There is an interesting story told by Herodotus about a Persian king's journey as he was on his way to invade Europe. It might be hard to believe or understand, but it says,

> When Xerxes the Persian king was on his way to invade Europe, he found a shelter there under the shade of a great plane tree. He so admired the tree and felt such gratitude to it that he decked it out with costly gifts, and left a personal bodyguard to care for it and to look after it.[123]

---

121 Clyde E. Fant and Mitchell G. Reddish, 300.
122 William Barclay, 67.
123 Ibid, 67.

The grounds surrounding Philadelphia were fertile and an agricultural dream. They were well known for the volume of grapes that were grown there. But unfortunately, as said before, the area was prone to earthquakes, and a massive earthquake that had severely damaged Sardis around AD 17 also caused extensive damage to Philadelphia, putting it back on its heels. "To help the city recover from this disaster, Emperor Tiberius remitted the tribute owed to Rome for a period of five years. In gratitude, Philadelphia took the name Neocaesarea and dedicated a temple to Tiberius."[124]

Still, the city took a long time to recover from this major earthquake and its many aftershocks. Eventually, under Roman rule, the city gradually came back to proper functionality. Like many of the other cities, Philadelphia had more than its fair share of Greek culture. All along the Roman post road were Hellenistic displays.

The Roman road was a major commercial artery that ran between Rome and the East. For a great portion of this fantastic thruway were magnificent buildings, including beautifully designed temples and public buildings. Philadelphia was strategically located and, as a result, eventually served as the gateway to the East, not only for the spread of Greek culture but also for the spread of missionary work. "Philadelphia had been built with the deliberate intention that it might become a missionary city."[125]

As is quite clear, with Philadelphia being one the seven churches that received a letter, Christianity became a major part of the life of the Philadelphians. So Christianity had its roots down into the late first century and continued to spread into the second century. Although Christianity thrived in Philadelphia, they suffered much at the hands of those who were more inclined to follow Hellenistic culture and the Jews who opposed their religious views.

---

124 Clyde E. Fant and Mitchell G. Reddish, 300.
125 William Barclay, 67

This church was characterized as having little strength after enduring much tribulation, persecution, and martyrdom. It appears that their persecutors also tried to weaken their faith and confidence in God by using those they punished as an example that others would be treated in the same manner.

> Early in the 2nd century, Ignatius, bishop of Antioch in Smyrna, passed through Philadelphia as a prisoner on his way to his martyrdom in Rome. Farther along on his journey, while at Troas, he wrote a letter to the church at Philadelphia encouraging the people to remain united and to support their bishop and other church leaders. Later (ca. 155 C.E), when Polycarp of Smyrna was martyred, some members of the church at Philadelphia were martyred at the same time. Although no direct evidence exists of Jewish inhabitants of Philadelphia in Hellenistic and Roman times, the book of Revelation gives indirect evidence. The Christians at Philadelphia had apparently been suffering in some way from the hands of the Jewish community in Philadelphia, a group that John describes pejoratively as "those of the synagogue of Satan who say that they are Jews and are not" (3:9).[126]

Not much is known about the origin of the church of Philadelphia, but there are a couple of speculations. It is believed by some that Christianity could have had its influence in a few ways that led to the establishment of the church in this city. It should also be remembered that the great influence of the apostle Paul spread throughout Asia Minor that led to the organizing of churches. There is one thought that people who heard Peter preaching at Pentecost and received the gospel in their own language could have returned home and started

---

126 Clyde E. Fant and Mitchell G. Reddish, 301.

a place of worship. These seven churches were not far from one another with large thruways where people went back and forth. And especially with miracles, signs, and wonders, there was the chance that there could have been spillover.

However, whatever the influence, the church of Philadelphia faced serious persecution and martyrdom but held strong. It became the church that kept the faith through perils and sword. In the face of adversity, this church kept the Word of God and held onto its faith, of which Christ commended it greatly and offered it great reward.

> The letter to Philadelphia is a letter of undiluted praise. In later days, when Islam swept across Asia Minor, for many a year Philadelphia stood as the last bastion of Christianity. When it fell, it did not fall through weakness or lack of courage; it fell because in the end it was actually betrayed by its fellow-Christians of Byzantium, who were jealous of its honor.[127]

This church symbolized one located in a hot spot, where there is severe hostility against Christianity, but it found the stamina to persevere. The apostle Paul mentioned in 2 Timothy: "It is a faithful saying: for if we be dead with him, we shall also life with him. If we suffer, we shall also reign with him: if we deny him, he also will deny us: if we believe not, yet he abideth faithful; he cannot deny himself" (2 Timothy 2:11–13). The church of Philadelphia epitomizes faithfulness and grace under pressure. One thing all of God's children can be assured of is that God rewards faithfulness.

Philadelphia was a place that had many gods and many religious persuasions. There were temples all along the streets, and Christianity was at a disadvantage, which resulted in persecutions and martyrdom.

---

[127] William Barclay, 71.

"Philadelphia had so many gods and so many temples that sometimes men called it 'Little Athens.' To walk through its temple-scattered streets was to be reminded of Athens, the center of worship of the Olympian gods (Barclay)".[128]

This was the nature and character of these provinces throughout Asia Minor that the church had to face constantly. While none can be justified for not holding to their faith, some even adopted the doctrines of the Nicolaitans, the church of Philadelphia was determined to not be another victim of failed faith and was willing to die for its conviction of salvation through, and only through, the shed blood of Christ, of which it was highly commended. They held fast to their faith under fire and did not abandon the trust they had in Christ. According to Dr. Peter Ruckman, this church

> Represents the church period from 1500 to 1900. This is the greatest period in history (as far as the church goes) for the Body of Christ. This is the only church of the seven churches that is not told to repent! This is the church that gets up and goes the way God intended for it to go … The movements of church forward is so powerful and so consistent that unsaved people think the world is getting better, so this is the age that teaches the theory of evolution as a fact![129]

The Letter to Philadelphia

As mentioned earlier of all the other churches, the letter was sent to the angel of the church of Philadelphia. It stated, "These things saith he that is holy, he that is true, he that hath the key of David,

---

128 David Guzik, Rev., 3.
129 Peter S. Ruckman, Loc. 1475.

he that openeth; and no man shutteth, and shutteth, and no man openeth."(Revelation 3:7) Christ introduced himself first as "holy"—pure and spotless in nature, character, sacred, and morally blameless. He also mentioned only two of his great attributes. These attributes do not refer to tendencies that Christ is pursuing or hoping to achieve. These attributes speak of his very being as holy, pure, and true.

The reference to his attributes does not suggest that this faithful church was not aware but rather as a reminder that gives a moral boost. This letter preempted what Christ intended to do for this faithful church and also his intent of consequence to those who had caused the saints much suffering. In the face of adversity, believers need to remember the example and instructions of Christ. As mentioned in John 16:33, "These things I have spoken unto you, that in me ye might have peace. In the world ye shall have tribulation: but be of good cheer; I have overcome the world."

Not only did Christ give them hope, he also set a great example of how to deal with trials and persecutions. Peter mentioned Christ and his approach to being reviled when he noted, "Who, when he was reviled, reviled not again; when he suffered, he threatened not; but committed himself to him that judgeth righteously" (1 Peter 2:23). Indeed, Christ judges righteously, and the Jews who were of the synagogue of Satan would soon find that out.

Christ established that he had the key of David. "This is a quotation from Isaiah 22:22, where it is a description of Eliakim, the faithful steward of Hezekiah. The king had given him the key so that none could gain admission to the royal palace and to the royal presence except through him alone."[130] This was symbolic and significant to the understanding of both the church and its adversaries who possibly heard of this letter. Having the key of David implied absolute authority and control. This was not the first time that Jesus declared his absolute

---

130 William Barclay, 72.

control. He told John in Revelation 1:18, "I am he that liveth, and was dead; and, behold I am alive for evermore, A-men; and have the keys of hell and death."(Revelation 1:18)

The authority of the key promised to open doors that no inferior authority could shut and, likewise, shut doors that no other could open. That Christ had the key of David could possibly have a twofold application. One, he is hailed as the Son of David who would sit on his throne, and two, it implies political authority of the king, who dictates the dos and don'ts.

> David, a man after God's heart, became king of the nation of Israel, and absolute ruler. It was he who had the power to allow men to enter or require them to leave the capital city, to maintain life or to deny it to those who opposed him and the nation he ruled. In those days anyone who held the keys to the city had the authority to open or close the gate, and no one else could overrule him, except the king of that city. It was also between the inner and outer gate into the city where the government of that city met. So in every respect the gate was vital to the city both in the day-to-day activity of entering, leaving and governing and for defence (Matt. 16:18).[131]

Christ knew their works, which led him to set before them an open door that no man could shut. In the minds of many, the open door has more than one interpretation. Fundamentally, however, the open door gives access and opportunity for them to spread the gospel of the grace of God and lead them into unchartered territories. As said

---

131 Peter Russell-Yarde, Letters to the Seven Churches, (Matters of Faith), Peter Russell-Yarde, 2013, Loc.1500.

Guzik, "Sometimes God sets an open door of evangelistic opportunity in front of us, but we don't see it."[132]

Christ knew the works of all the other six churches, but there is something special about this church. Their lives were reflected in the gospel of Matthew: "Blessed are ye, when men shall revile you, and persecute you, and say all manner of evil against you falsely, for my sake" (Matthew 5:11).

Their moment of rejoicing came early when they were commended for not losing faith. Nor did they deserve the persecution and death they experienced. "Historically, 'the church in Philadelphia' is the church of the Reformation and the missionary church of the 18th through the 20th centuries. The dates 1500–1900 A.D. would generally encompass this Philadelphian church."[133]

This church received no criticism but was noted that with "little strength" it had kept the Word of God and had not denied his name. The reference to "little strength" could be viewed from the cup half empty or half full. One could view this as very weak, but they had enough strength to hold on.

On the other hand, it could be viewed as strong enough to resist all that the Devil threw at it and survive, in testimony and doctrine. "Which is a manifest token of the righteous judgment of God, that ye may be counted worthy of the kingdom of God for which ye also suffer: seeing it is a righteous thing with God to recompense tribulation to them that trouble you" (2 Thessalonians 1:5–6).

They were able to stand up against the principalities and powers, fighting with spiritual weapons and pulling down the strongholds of the Enemy. God rewards faithfulness and, as a result, was ready to recompense the enemies as their just reward. The turnaround is that God promised to make the imposters humble before the Philadelphian

---

132 David Guzik, Rev., 3.
133 Geroge Grace, 44.

saints. Finis Dake makes ten predictions, four of which were fulfilled and six yet to be.

> I will expose all liars, (v 9) I will humble them before you; I will confirm my love of you to them; I will keep you from persecution (v 10) I will come quickly (v 11; 1:7; 19:11); I will make you a pillar in the temple of my God, (v 12; Gal. 2:9) Thou will never go out, but will always have a safe dwelling place, (v 12) I will give you God's name (v 12) I will give you the name of the new Jerusalem, (v 12; Rev. 21:2, 9–10) I will give you my new name.[134]

The confidence of the church of Philadelphia concerning its persecution and suffering had its root in Christ's promise, "Behold, I will make them of the synagogue of Satan which say they are Jews and are not, but do lie; behold, I will make them to come and worship before thy feet, and to know that I have loved you" (Revelation 3:9). Christ's promise of humiliation to this group of imposters who pretended to be Jews but by character were Satan worshippers created a long-awaited sense of vindication within the church.

The Synagogue of Satan

The "synagogue of Satan" suggests that these people were pretenders in some way. They pretended to be who they were not; they lived by a name, but their character and way of life did not hold true to their profession. There are a number of thoughts concerning the "synagogue of Satan".

---

134 Finis Dake, Comments on Rev. 3, the letter p.

i. Those enemies are described to be such as said they were Jews, but lied in saying so—pretended to be the only and peculiar people of God. But were really the synagogue of Satan. Assemblies that worship God in spirit and truth are the Israel of God; assemblies that either worship false gods, or the true God in a false manner, are the synagogue of Satan: Though they may profess to be the only people of God, their profession is a lie.[135]

ii. Apparently, the Christians in Philadelphia were persecuted by Jewish people (the synagogue). However, these persecuting Jews were Jews in name only (who say they were Jews and are not, but lie). In fact, they have no spiritual connection to Abraham or to the people of faith.[136]

iii. In v. 9, "the synagogue of Satan" reappears, as was previously seen in Revelation 2:9. Once again, these are those "which say they are Jews, and are not." A-millennial theologians negate them to "the Church," i.e., they may be spiritual Jews (Romans 8), but they are not Jews according to the flesh! God is not yet done with the nation of Israel (Romans 9–11).[137]

iv. We found this same bunch of liars in the Smyrna period, A.D. 150 to A.D. 325 (Rev. 2:9). Smyrna had this bunch of people in it who claimed that they were really Jews,

---

135 Matthew Henry, 1133
136 David Guzik, Rev. 3.
137 George Grace, 44.

and that God was all through with the physical Jews, and they claimed to be the true successors to Israel, and taught Postmillennial doctrine. These "birds" pop up again in Revelation 3:9, in the Reformation period. They claim that they are Jews, when they are actually Romans. The claim that they replace Israel, when they have done nothing but steal from Israel. They claim that the Kingdom of Heaven and the Kingdom of God are different. They are the same clique of Postmillennial robbers who have been perverting the word of God since the Acts of the Apostles.[138]

It is clear that there have been, and still are, differences of opinion concerning the synagogue of Satan. However, whatever conclusion one arrives at, the consequences remain the same: Christ promised their personal humiliation by worshipping at the feet of the saints of Philadelphia. The intent was to prove to them that Christ really loved his church, which he had "purchased with his own blood"(Acts 20:28). In other words, what Christ was saying in essence is that those who thought themselves high would be brought low. "I will make them to come and worship before thy feet."(Revelation 3:9)

The word that Christ used for worship was *pros-koo-neh-o*, which means to "kiss, like a dog licking his master's hand; to fawn or crouch, to prostrate oneself in homage, to do reverence or adore."[139] This was one of the most humiliating things Christ could have promised: that their enemies would prostrate before the church, licking their feet like dogs.

---

[138] Peter S. Ruckman, Loc. 1490.

[139] Brian Thomas Webb, Strong's Concordance for iPhone version 1.5.3, Copyright 2009.

> They shall worship at thy feet; not pay a religious and divine honor to the church itself, not to the ministry of it, but shall be convinced that they have been in the wrong, that this church is in the right and is beloved of Christ, and they shall desire to be taken into communion with her and that they may worship the name of God after the same manner.[140]

He expressed his love for this church because "thou hast kept the word of my patience." (Revelation 3:10) They kept the word and doctrine, which caused them to be persecuted, but they were patient in tribulation. They found a way to rejoice in tribulation and remained hopeful. The words of Isaiah literally had its fulfillment in their lives: "But they that wait upon the Lord shall renew their strength; they shall mount up with wings like eagles; they shall run, and not be weary; and they shall walk and not faint"(Isaiah 40:31).

Christ's promise of reward is that he would keep them "from the hour of temptation."(Revelation 3:10) This hour of temptation is said to be coming upon the whole world to try those who dwell upon the earth. This statement is not agreed on by all theologians. Some think of it as a prophetic declaration while others see it as troubled times upon the churches in John's day. For example, David Guzik says, "Most Bible scholars see this hour of trial as a prophetic reference to Messianic woes, the Great Tribulation, which precede Jesus' earthly kingdom. Jesus promises to keep these Christians from that hour of trial".[141] On the other hand, Finis Dake has another take on the use of the word *tribulation*. He says, "Not the future tribulation of Daniel's 70th week, but an hour of tribulation upon the churches in John's day."[142]

---

140 Matthew Henry,1133.

141 David Guzik, Rev. 3.

142 Finis Dake, Rev., 3 note s.

One could justify this in either times, whether it was in John's day or a reference to Daniel's seventieth week. Certainly for the premillennialist, the church in general will not go through the great tribulation, neither in whole or in part because God hath not appointed his children unto wrath. "For God hath not appointed us to wrath, but to obtain salvation by our Lord Jesus Christ" (1 Thessalonians 5:9). On the other hand, his promise to bring their persecutors to worship at their feet could mean that they would never again experience the level of temptation they went through. Whichever way it is interpreted, the meaning is the same: Christ would prevent them from the hour of temptation. And if it is for their faithfulness, it would make sense that they would experience deliverance from what they had been going through, as well as for their patience and keeping the word of Christ in their hearts.

While Christ promises to deliver his children from the hour of temptation, the opposite is true of those who "dwell upon the earth." Those who "dwell on the earth" suggests those who are not in Christ, whose names are not written in the Book of Life as John mentioned: "And they that dwell on the earth shall wonder, whose names were not written in the book of life from the foundation of the world, when they behold the beast that was, and is not, and yet is" (Revelation 17:8). So then the idea of those who dwell on the earth is synonymous with the lost because believers will live with Christ in heaven. "Christians are different. Though we walk on this earth, our dwelling place is in heaven. We have been seated in heavenly places in Jesus."[143]

It is stated profoundly in Colossians 3:3–4 that the believer's life is hidden in Christ: "For ye are dead, and your life is hid with Christ in God. When Christ, who is our life shall appear, then shall ye also appear with him in glory." The church was admonished to hold fast the Word and promise that they had and never allow anyone to take

---

143 David Guzik, Rev. 3.

their crown. Steadfastness and determination are implied in order to not lose their crown.

They were reminded to reflect on how they got where they were: to hold onto God's grace, the truth of God's Word, and the doctrines they knew. Because they were commended, rewarded, and given a great promise, they should never become complacent. The Devil is always like a roaring lion, seeking whom he may devour. The suddenness of Christ's return was emphasized in the admonition. No man knows the day or the hour of his coming. Behold I come quickly, does not suggest immediacy but sudden, an uncertainty of time. As a result, all generations are implored in the same manner to anticipate the coming of the Lord at all times. Therefore, it is absolutely crucial not to allow one to take your crown.

The parable of the good man recorded in Luke 12:39–40 is a prime example: "And this know, that if the good man of the house had known what hour the thief would come, he would have watched, and not have suffered his house to be broken through. Be ye therefore ready also: for the Son of man cometh at an hour when ye think not." Let no one seize or remove your crown! The word Christ used for "crown" is the Greek *stef-an-os*, which speaks of a chaplet or a badge of royalty.[144] No Christian would want to lose is or her crown of victory; therefore, it should be held fast.

> That no one take your crown: if they fail to hold fast, their crown might be given to another. The idea is not that it might be stolen by another, but given. This is not a crown of royalty, given because of royal birth. This is a crown of victory. Jesus encourages His saints to finish their course with victory, to "play the second half" just as strongly as they "played the first half." Never forget that the man most

---

144 Brian Thomas Webb.

likely to steal your crown is yourself. "Keep thy heart with all diligence, for out of it are the issues of life" (Proverbs 4:23). You are in no greater danger from anyone or anything than from yourself (Havner).[145]

One cannot underestimate the expressions made here by Christ himself about the danger of losing one's crown. The reason for losing it is solely on one's not holding fast to the Word. "What would be the object of this statement if there was no possibility of a Christian losing his crown?"[146] This is also supported by Revelation 2:10. It behooves all Christians to be faithful till death to be assured of the coveted crown promised to those who are faithful until death.

Christians cannot afford to carelessly and casually hold onto this priceless treasure and gift of God's grace and love. This incomparable, unmerited, unearned favor must be viewed in light of Revelation 2:3–4, where the Lord admonished and warned the church of Ephesus who had "left their first love" to repent or have their candlesticks removed.

A Pillar in the Temple

The great promises continued, however, but not without requisites. "Him that overcometh" will be made a pillar in the temple of God. That is a profound statement with the common understanding of a literal pillar in the physical temple. The word used for "overcometh," first of all, is the word *nik-ah-o*, which means "to subdue, literally or figuratively; it is to conquer, overcome, prevail, or get the victory."[147]

---

145 David Guzik, Rev. 3.
146 Finis Dake, Rev. 3, u.
147 Brian Thomas Webb.

In other words, if one falls victim and loses to the enemy, he or she cannot be a pillar, the fortifying source of the temple.

In this church, Christ promised that he would personally make the overcomers a pillar in the temple of God. For those who understand construction, especially of large buildings with many floor levels, the columns, or pillars, are the most important to the stability and durability of that building. When the pillars are firmly in place, the building will stand many storms. With the building fitted firmly on the pillars, most additional partitions can be removed and the building will still stand. It is the reason that the apostle Paul stated in Ephesians 2:20 that the temple has its foundation on the apostles and prophets with Christ as the chief cornerstone.

The pillars are similarly important. So when Jesus used the metaphor of the overcomers as the pillar in the temple of God, they immediately understood what he was saying. Because they had been through much and kept the faith, they had proven themselves reliable and able to hold the forth through trials.

Samson understood that the strength of a building lies solely on the pillars, which is why he asked the lad to allow him to feel the pillars of the building where the Philistines lay who had gouged out his eyes. "And Samson said unto the lad that held him by the hand, suffer me that I may feel the pillars whereupon the house standeth, that I may lean upon them" (Judges 16:26cf). Samson took hold of the two middle pillars upon which the house stood and, holding on with both hands, cried unto the Lord to allow his revenge, and he brought the house down by removing the pillars. So while this was a symbolic and metaphoric use of a pillar, it left great confidence in the minds of the believers.

> For people who had experienced firsthand the instability and impermanence of buildings during a severe earthquake and who at times had to flee their homes and city to keep from being injured or killed by tumbling buildings, the promise

that they would be a pillar (of strength) and would never have to go out of the temple would indeed be good news. [148]

The next promise, that they would "go no more out," suggests there would be no more instability for the overcomers. Instead, they would have a place of permanence and peace of mind. Some believe this promise was futuristic and speaks of the final victory of believers, but it doesn't matter because, in their minds, there was lasting confidence in the promises of Christ.

Christ continued to lavish unheard of things onto those who had struggled with their own identity and were rejected by those who said they were Jews and considered unfavorable to even mention the name of God. Now they were assured by Christ that they would bear the name of his God, the name of the city of God, and a new name from Christ himself.

One can only imagine that these are symbolic to a medal of honor given by Christ himself. This has no less permanence than how he began his introduction to them that the doors he opens no man can shut and is an affront to those Jews who lambasted, ridiculed, tortured, and even killed them for the word of their testimony.

Christ promised that their persecutors would worship them and kiss their feet. At the same time, they would know that the name of God, the New Jerusalem, and a name known only by Christ and given to these overcomers would be enough to haunt their enemies. The Devil and the beast would brand those who worship them with their own mark of ownership for doom (Revelation 13:16–17; 14:11; 19:20; 20:4). Clearly, none will be left without a mark of identity; sadly for some, their mark will seal their doom, while for the overcomers, it will be for their eternal rejoicing. The letter also concludes that everyone who has ears should hear what the Spirit says to the churches. This is crucial in every way!

---

148 Clyde E. Fant, and Mitchell G. Reddish, 301.

CHAPTER 10

THE CHURCH OF LAODICEA

The church of Laodicea is the last of the seven churches but is in no way the least. It is instead the most interesting among them because its marks and characteristics are unquestionable when compared to today's contemporary church. The similarities are inseparable, as will be seen further in this study. Laodicea, like all the other churches, was located in the far west of Asia Minor.

It is important to know that there were a number of cities named Laodicea in Syria and Asia Minor, but this city was strategically located within the confines of Phrygia and Lydia and no doubt had the characteristics that God foresaw within the church at the end. To better understand which of the Laodicean cities were mentioned, it was identified as "Laodicea at Lycum."

It was located south of Philadelphia and about ninety miles east of Ephesus. There would have been a straight line between Ephesus and Laodicea had there been a line drawn and had God chosen to make it the second church. However, the seven churches formed the shape of a horseshoe, and Laodicea was in direct view of Ephesus. Ephesus was the first city, and Laodicea was the last.

This city had a few name changes prior to being named Laodicea.

> After having been successively called Disopolis and Rhoas, it was named Laodicea in honor of Laodice, the wife of Antiochus II (261–246 B.C.), who rebuild it. It was destroyed by an earthquake (A.D. 66, or earlier) and rebuilt by Marcus Aurelius. It was a seat of a Christian church (Col. 2:1; 4:13; 15–16; Rev. 1:11).[149]

This city has much history from both a location standpoint (culture and tradition) and a religious one. This ancient city had great commercial success—one reason because of its strategic location. Like many of the other cities, its commercial strength was a key portion of its wealth, and its location put it at a vantage point, as it was positioned at the junction of two major roadways. These two roads "ran from the Aegean coast near Ephesus through the Meander River valley and on to the Euphrates, and another that ran from Pergamum to Sardis and then to Perga and Attalia (modern Antalya)."[150]

One of the notable things about Laodicea is that around 80–50 BC, this city was well known for its judicial administrative power, which attracted the governor of Cilicia, Cicero, to practice administering justice there around 50 BC.

Another interesting thing about this city is that it lost a bid to build a temple for the worship of Emperor Tiberius due to its weak economic standing. As years went by, the economy grew to a much higher level. However, the entire Asia Minor was in an earthquake-

---

149 Merrill F. Unger, The New Unger's Bible Dictionary, p. 756, Loc.37507.
150 Clyde E. Fant and Mitchell G. Robinson, 233.

prone zone, and time after time, these cities moved forward and then backward because of devastating earthquakes. This was true Laodicea and the surrounding areas. It seems they made three steps forward and two backward. However, Laodicea had a lot of pride and refused to take handouts from Rome in its rebuilding stage. They persevered and rebuilt from their own resources.

> Laodicea was famous in the ancient world for its raven-black wool, which was especially soft, and for its textile industry. According to Strabo (*Geography* 12.8.20), a great medical school was located in (or near) Laodicea, a claim that is supported by coins from Laodicea that bear the names of leading physicians of the school. The city was apparently also a banking center, as Cicero mentions that when he arrived in Laodicea he cashed his letters of credit in the city (Epistulae ad familiars 3.5.4).[151]

As a wealthy, commercially strong city, Laodicea had a good export system in place as it was known and prized for a popular eye salve, fine wool, and other woven materials.

All of these small cities were vulnerable to attack from their enemies, but Laodicea was even more vulnerable because of its poor water system. Its enemies could cause even more destruction by disrupting their water supply system. Unlike some of the other cities that had been taken over by different commanders time and again, Laodicea seemed to have avoided some of the devastating conflicts through accommodating conversations and negotiations. It is fair to say, then, that it avoided much enemy destruction. But unfortunately it couldn't avoid or negotiate with the vicious earthquakes it experienced.

---

151 Ibid, 233.

A lot more could be said about this historically prominent city, although it lies in ruin and has not received as much attention as the other ancient cities. However, its prominence and historic importance as it pertains to the church historically and contemporarily has not diminished. The church of Laodicea received a lot of attention then as well as now.

The Laodicean church epitomizes where the church stands today, at least in a broad or general sense. Observing the characteristics of that church and comparing them to what is obvious today confirms the belief that while these churches had literal and historic existence, a larger picture reflects the church in its existence on earth. Sadly, the church today looks like the Laodicean church. This is not to say that all of the body of Christ is lukewarm or driven by wealth and self-gratification, but almost everywhere one looks, there is the resemblance of the church of Laodicea. If this is true, and the church is at a crucial place, we need to pay special attention to its status.

The reputation of this church is not a pleasant end for the church. God did not plan it to be so, but because of his foreknowledge and omniscience, he knew it would be; hence the letter to the churches and the warning to listen to the voice of the Spirit or face the consequences.

This church is mentioned by the apostle Paul in Colossians a number of times, showing his concern and, likewise, sending greetings. He told the church at Colossae to read his epistle to the Laodicean church and sent them what should be read at Colossae as well. "And when this epistle is read among you, cause that it be read also in the church of the Laodiceans; and that ye likewise read the epistle from Laodicea" (Colossians 4:16).

> The earliest reference to a Christian presence in Laodicea comes from the book of Colossians in the New Testament. The people in the church at Colossae are told to read "the letter from Laodicea," and the Colossian letter is to be read "in the church of the Laodiceans" (4:16). During the latter

> part of the 2nd century, one of the Laodicean Christians, a man named Sagaris, who was a bishop of the church at Laodicea, was killed as a Christian martyr (Eusebius, Ecclesiastical History 4.26.3; 5.24.5). In the 4th century an important church council met at Laodicea.[152]

If there is a true example of types and shadows, or symbolism, the church of Laodicea is the true shadow of what is seen in the church today. It is only God who knows all and can see from time to eternity past and future who could foresee what would be unfolding today.

This last of the seven churches represents the last of the church age and is a bad reflection on the teachings and doctrines of Christ. This reputation should be avoided in the church at every cost. It is apparent that almost everything this church did didn't fall in line with God's will.

> We now come to the last and worst of all the seven Asian churches, the reverse of the church of Philadelphia; for, as there was nothing reproved in that, here is nothing commended in this, and yet this was one *of the seven golden candlesticks*, for a corrupt church may still be a church.[153]

God indeed has given the church today many examples, both good and bad. They are given pointers so they can know both and see God's reaction to faithfulness and failure. There are many interesting things about this church then and now that will be examined.

> The word "Laodicean" means, the "rights or justices of the people"—literally, the civil rights of the people. The name

---

152 Ibid, 234.
153 Matthew Henry, 1134.

suggests a democratic church that no longer follows spiritual leaders. Historically, this is the last church on Earth before the return of our Lord Jesus Christ. This is the Church Age we live in today in the 21st Century: the apostate, dead, lukeward, neo-orthodox, ecumenical, charismatic, socialistic "hodgepodge" called "The Church."[154]

Nothing good has been said about this church, especially when contrasted with the church of Philadelphia. They seem to have taken on the persona of the city and decided to bask in the glory of its wealth, not realizing the difference between spiritual wealth and financial wealth.

As mentioned earlier, Laodicea refused the help of the Romans in the rebuilding process of the city after a devastating earthquake in AD 60. The people were proud and believed themselves as "wanting nothing" and exercised self-reliance. This is the same attitude the church exhibited when Christ observed it in Revelation 3:18, "Because thou sayest, I am rich, and increased with goods, and have need of nothing." Their braggadocio attitude placed them on a self-built pedestal of materialistic prominence but spiritual deflation. They were not focused on spiritual things but fully indulged in materialistic gratification, forgetting what was required of the church and where the church's wealth really lies. It found itself in a very pitiable and compromised position, making itself comfortable with the natural things while totally forgetting the spiritual.

It had gotten so bad that Christ concluded that he was not even on the inside when they gathered together. It would be safe to say that while their hearts were lifted up with pride and they had more than they could consume by the flesh, they were spiritually malnourished to the point of death, yet no one knew it.

---

154 George Grace, 47.

About thirty years before John sent the "revelation" letter, Laodicea had been destroyed by an earthquake, but the wealthy—and possibly arrogant—city declined Rome's offer of financial assistance in the rebuilding process. Apparently the city already felt—as the church did later—that they "had need of nothing" from any source outside themselves. As for "religion," there were the pagan gods. Principally centering around the Temple of Zeus. The church at Laodicea is thought to have been established by Epaphras, apparently an associate of Paul's. (See Colossians 4:12–15.) As in other places, there may have been Jews at Laodicea who were present in Jerusalem at the feast of Pentecost in A.D. 33, and were converted by Peter's preaching ... The Thomson Bible Survey says: "The wealth and worldly prestige led to an increased licentiousness and compromise on moral issues ... The church adopted a spirit of accommodation and of broad toleration, and was entirely self-satisfied. Proud of its prestige in the city, it had 'need of nothing' in its own eye. Today, the ruins of the old city surround a village named Eski-Hissar. The modern city of Denizli, more or less taking Laodicea's place, lies a few miles to the south."[155]

So it seems that the Laodiceans were so full of themselves that they concluded they needed help from no one, neither from Rome nor, by their behavior, from God. That, however, would be to their own peril unless they quickly realized their depravity and repented. Every man is right in his own eyes and justified in his own conceit. And the church of Laodicea was as conceited as it gets.

---

155 White Wing Publishing House and Press, 119.

The Letter to Laodicea

This letter is the last of the seven letters and is the most distasteful of them and, to a certain extent, the worst rebuke meted out to any of the churches. Like all the other letters, it was addressed to the "angel of the church" of the Laodiceans. It is noted that Christ introduced himself to all the churches in a different manner based on their behavior and their experiences.

Paul suggests that "I am made all things to all men, that I might by all means save some" (1 Corinthians 9:22). "These things saith the Amen" is an interesting way to make an introduction, especially using the word *amen*, as it is transliterated from the Hebrew to mean "truth, affirmation, or certainty."[156] To a further extent, the word suggests, "So be it; it's done; I approve."[157] This is not the first time Christ is mentioned as the "Amen," as is seen in 2 Corinthians 1:20, "For all the promises of God in him are yea, and in him Amen, unto the glory of God." This verse is saying that all the promises of God are truth, so be it, and it's done.

Not only are the promises the truth, but, likewise, the witness is true. Jesus told Nicodemus, "We speak of what we do know," and for Christ to introduce himself to the Laodicean church as the Amen, the faithful and true witness, he immediately lays the foundation for his findings and testimony as the true witness of their lifestyle and behavior. Neither of these two qualities could be said of the Laodicean church. They were not faithful, and they were not true. They were not even having a relationship with him, because he suggested later in the letter that he was outside knocking, trying to come in if anyone would have let him in. He reminded them that he is the "beginning of the creation of God," as stated in John 1, and is the source of all

---

156 Brian Thomas Webb, Strong's Concordance for iPhone version 1.5.3, Copyright 2009.

157 Ibid.

beginnings and the one who controls the end. All things were made by him and all things are known by him. "I know thy works," as he knew all the works of the other churches.

Lukewarm

Now, the first thing Jesus told the Laodiceans about themselves was that they were neither cold nor hot. This rings a bell in the minds of everyone. Again, Christ used their own personal experiences to give them the big picture of how he feels about them. They were lukewarm! There are a number of factors to consider in this statement. The word used for "lukewarm" is "*khlee-ar-os,* which means to be warm or tepid."[158] Tepid suggests that they lacked passion, force, or zest and were marked by the absence of enthusiasm, conviction, or interest. To tell them that they were lukewarm reminds them of their own insipid water supply. Because of how it was carried into the city, it was apparently exposed to the elements. So by the time it got into the city, the water was warm and not palatable. If water is cold, it is wonderful for quenching one's thirst. However, if it is hot, it would be good for tea. Spiritually, if one is cold, one might realize it and make the effort to change. But if one is warm, he or she is comfortable enough to remain as he or she is, not wanting anything.

Anyone who has taken a glass of water to drink, hoping it was cold but finding it lukewarm, can remember spewing it out with disappointment and disgust. The word Jesus used for "spew" is *em-eh-o,* which means to vomit.[159] David Guzik gives four interesting thoughts on this lukewarm position:

---

158 Ibid.
159 Ibid.

What Jesus wants to change in us as much as anything is the deceptive playing of the middle, trying to please both the world and Jesus.

i. I could wish that you were cold or hot points to another aspect of lukewarmness, as a picture of ourselves. "Hot water heals, cold water refreshes, but lukewarm water is useless for either purpose." (Morris) It's as if Jesus says, "if you were hot or cold I could do something with you. But because you are neither, I will do nothing." The lukewarm Christian has enough of Jesus to satisfy a craving for religion, but not enough for eternal life.

ii. The thief on the cross was cold towards Jesus and clearly saw his need. The Apostle John was not towards Jesus and enjoyed an intimate relationship of love. But Judas was lukewarm, following Jesus enough to be considered a disciple, but not giving his heart to Jesus in fullness.

iii. Deep down, there is no one more miserable than the lukewarm Christian is. They have too much of the world to be happy in Jesus, but too much of Jesus to be happy in the world.

iv. But how could Jesus say, I could wish that you were cold? We know His deepest desire is that they be hot, with an on-fire love for Him (Revelation 3:19, where the word zealous is associated with this same word hot). Yet if they would not be hot, Jesus prefers cold rather than lukewarm. "So the Lord is saying, 'if instead of being lukewarm, you were so cold that you should feel that coldness, then the very feeling of your

> need might drive you to the true warmth, but now in your lukewarmness, you have just enough to protect yourselves against a feeling of need'" (Barnhouse).[160]

The major problem this church faced was that it was comfortable with its material wealth. "Because thou sayest, I am rich (ploo-see-os) wealthy, abounding with riches, and increased with goods, and have need of nothing."(Revelation 3:17) speaks of the narrowness of their minds and where their treasure lay. Jesus said, "A man's life consisteth not in the abundance of the things which he possesseth" (Luke 12:15b).

Even Solomon with all his wealth, gold, silver, treasure—more than he could consume or even account of—wives, and concubines, recognized that those things in themselves were not life, and neither did they bring spiritual gratification. Then he rightly said, "Then I looked on all the works that my hands had wrought, and on the labour that I had laboured to do: and, behold, all was vanity and vexation of spirit, and there was no profit under the sun" (Ecclesiastes 2:11). Jesus again warns against having one's treasure locked away on earth where moth and dust doth corrupt.

Fivefold Indictment

Christians are always reminded that treasures on earth are temporal and prone to be lost, but those stowed away in heaven are eternal and cannot be taken or tarnished by external elements.

> Lay not up for yourselves treasures upon earth, where moth and rust doth corrupt, and where thieves break through and

---

160 David Guzik, Rev. 3.

> steal: but lay up for yourselves treasures in heaven, where neither moth nor rust doth corrupt, and where thieves do not break through nor steal. For where your treasure is, there will your heart be also. (Matthew 6:19–21)

The church of Laodicea thought it needed nothing because its treasure chest was filled with earthly goods. The danger was they were in a dilemma and were oblivious to it. They knew not that they were wretched, pitiable, and miserable. If someone has to tell you that you are miserable, you are in a predicament. Not only that, they were wretched and miserable, and in the eyes of Christ, they were poor. They were in dire straits; they were poor, next to being beggars, like paupers. They were blind, as they couldn't see where they were, and were clueless about the quagmire they found themselves in. If that was not bad enough, Jesus told them that they were naked and didn't know. They were proud of themselves but were to pitied by those who could see how far they were from God.

> They were naked, without clothing and without house or harbour for their souls. They were without clothing, had neither the garment of justification nor the garment of sanctification. Their nakedness both of guilt and pollution had no covering. They lay always exposed to sin and shame. Their righteousness were but filthy rags; they were rags, and would not cover them, filthy rags, and would not defile them. And they were naked, without house or harbour, for they were without God, and he has been the dwelling-place of his people in all ages; in him alone the soul of man can find rest, and safety, and all suitable accommodations. The riches of the body will not enrich the soul; the sight of the body will not enlighten the soul; the most convenient house of the body will not afford rest nor safety for nor safety to the soul. The soul is a different thing from the body, and

must have accommodations suitable to its nature, or else in the midst of bodily prosperity it will be wretched and miserable.[161]

The Laodicean church was called into account by Christ because of its indulgence in material wealth while its spiritual condition was desperate. In other words, Christ recommended that they come to the realization of their spiritual poverty in order to be rich. The first step in making correction is realizing that one is going down the wrong path.

This was the moment of consciousness for the Laodicean church to put its trust in Christ and not in its wealth. Material prosperity and spiritual poverty is to the detriment of every church because a church's relationship with Christ is not dependent on materialistic power. "Wherefore let him that thinketh he standeth take heed lest he fall" (1 Corinthians 10:12). David Guzik tells an interesting story of a man who had a brief conversation with a pope during the Renaissance Papacy.

> Often, material riches are acquired and maintained at the expense of true spiritual riches. In the glory days of the Renaissance Papacy, a man walked with the pope and marveled at the splendors and riches of the Vatican. The pope told him, "we no longer have to say what Peter told the lame man: 'silver and gold have I none.'" His companion replied, "but neither can you say, 'rise up and walk.'"[162]

Although this is humorous, it brings to light the reality of the dangers of putting material gain over the work and manifestation of the Holy

---

161 Matthew Henry, 1136.
162 David Guzik, Rev. 2.

Spirit. Still, one cannot say or justify that a church less focused on material wealth is automatically a spiritually strong church. However, it can be said that a church whose complete focus is on gold and silver and not on intimacy with Christ is in danger of spiritual death. It is sad when a church cannot see that it has fallen into the valley of spiritual death. The admonition to the Laodiceans was that they buy of Christ "gold tried in fire."(Revelation 3:18)

"Gold tried in fire" is symbolic to pureness and white raiment (pureness or holiness), which is Christ's righteousness, that would cover their nakedness. Gold tried in fire suggests purity and also teaches that going through trying times will make you stronger and better once the process is completed. "That the trying of your faith, being much more precious than of gold that perisheth, though it be tried with fire, might be found unto praise and honour and glory at the appearing of Jesus Christ" (1 Peter 1:7). Gold is not at its purest point until it has been tried in fire.

In regard to what Christ told the Laodicean church, their gold would compare to that which had only being mined but had not been processed. They needed to anoint their eyes with eye salve so they might see, as they were spiritually blind.

What this desperate and destitute church needed to know was that Christ rebuked it because he loved them. And like a father who wishes his children well, he chastened them for their own long-term benefit. However, the call was not just to recognize where they were but also to repent. Jesus did not lose his love for this church because of its condition. Rather he rebuked them to change and do better.

Christ Outside Knocking

A look at Revelation 3:20 is an indictment against this church. With all that they were doing on the inside, Christ was saying he was outside, knocking. "Behold I stand at the door and knock" has always indicated that Christ is knocking at the door of sinners' hearts, waiting for entrance. While it is true that Christ knocks at the heart of the sinners, it must be noted here that this was a church.

If one believes that it is unfortunate for Christ to knock and seek entrance in the sinner's heart, imagine him saying this to this church. When gathered for what should have been worship, Christ was saying that he needed entrance; that he was standing on the outside, knocking, hoping that someone would open unto him. Christ was not just standing at the portal of entry; he was knocking and hoping that someone would have the spiritual discernment to hear him knocking.

Unlike the letter that was sent directly to the angel of the church, this call is a general call to anyone in this church who would open the door. This metaphor suggests that somebody needed to come to his or her senses and realize that material strength but spiritual destitution would be the death of the church. As mentioned previously, Christ's love for the church had not changed, as referenced here in verse 19, "As many as I love, I rebuke and chasten."

In other words, Christ was making clear that admonishing them was for their benefit. They thought they were well clothed, but in his eyes, they were naked. They thought they had plenty, but they were poor. They thought they had it made, but they were miserable and wretched. And the danger was they could not see this. Christ was not knocking as a stranger but as a familiar person. Hence, he stated, "If any man hear my voice,"(Revelation 3:20) and opens the door, this would give Christ access to come in and sit with them at the table.

In verse 20, the risen Christ says, "Behold I stand at the door and knock." There are two possible meanings here.

> i. It may mean that the end is near, and that the new age is about to dawn (cp. Mark 13:29; James 5:9). The early Church was dominated by the thought of the Second Coming; and this may be a summons to be ready before the King and Judge arrives upon the

earth. It is always true that eternity is knocking at the door of time.

ii. More likely the thought is that Jesus Christ is knocking at the door of our hearts, because He wishes us to receive Him as our guest. R. H. Charles makes the beautiful suggestion that the words come from the Love song of Solomon: "It is the voice of my beloved that knocketh saying, Open to me, my sister, my love, my dove" (Song of Solomon 5:2). It is the picture of Christ, the lover of the souls of men, knocking at the door of the human heart.[163]

The knocking is for sinners as well as for saints! It is more unfortunate, however, for Christ to be knocking at the door of his children, beseeching someone, anyone, to open the door. It can be understood when it is a sinner's door that is locked against (Christ coming in. But for his children's door to be locked against him, it is unprecedented. However, the message goes out to all: "Today if ye will hear his voice, harden not your hearts, as in the provocation" (Hebrews 3:15). The most important thing that needed to happen for the door to be opened was for somebody to hear Christ's voice.

But hearing God's voice does not necessarily cause one to immediately open his door, as Adam did the opposite. "And he said, I heard thy voice in the garden: and I was afraid, because I was naked, and I hid myself" (Genesis 3:10). The guilty conscience often drives one away from Christ if one's inclination is not to repent. That's one of the reasons why Christ's first call is to repentance, followed by restoration.

---

163 William Barclay, 88.

He promised this church that if he came in, he would sit and sup with them. Whatever the struggles or challenges one or a church faces, God through Christ will reward those who overcome. "To him that overcometh will I grant to sit with me in my throne, even as I also overcame, and am set down with my Father in his throne" (Revelation 3:21).

This is an elaborate offer considering that Jesus compared the promise to the overcomer to his victory over sin, death, and hell. Those who conquer or prevail over the Enemy's ploy will be rewarded in similar manner, just as Jesus overcame and is now sitting on his Father's throne. However, it is important to not forget that Christ is indeed God and is not a beneficiary of the things of heaven, but rather he positioned himself in human form for his people to understand the comparison. It also shows that those who have become lukewarm can be restored, and those who have lost their way can find the way back if they realize that they have lost their way, repent, and turn back to the Lord.

The same principle was applied in Zechariah when God offered restoration to Judah. The message he gave to Zechariah was one of hope and restoration, but the onus was totally on the people to return. God would keep his promises if the people would listen and respond.

> Therefore say to them, Thus saith the LORD of hosts; turn ye unto me, saith the LORD of hosts, and I will turn unto you, saith the LORD of hosts. Be ye not as your fathers, unto whom the former prophets have cried, saying, Thus saith the LORD of hosts; turn ye now from your evil doings; but they did not hear, nor hearken unto me, saith the LORD. (Zechariah 1:3–4)

God has always been willing to forgive all who repent and turn from their evil ways. David realized that God would not despise one who had a broken and contrite heart, as he stated in Psalm 51:16–17,

"For thou desirest not sacrifice; else would I give it: thou delightest not in burnt offering. The sacrifices of God are a broken spirit: a broken and a contrite heart, O God, thou wilt not despise." God will always guarantee his action and reaction because he honors his Word above his name.

Thus the conclusion of the letter to the seventh of the seven churches. The letter ended like all the other letters: "He that hath an ear, let him hear what the Spirit saith unto the churches."(Revelation 3:22) The Spirit searches all things, the deep things of God, and he knows the hidden things of the heart, and, yes, he knows the mind of God. Therefore, whatever the Spirit saith to the churches are the exact things Christ and God are saying.

CHAPTER 11

THE GLORY SHALL RETURN TO THE CHURCH

As we look at the church today, where it is in the mind of some, and what it is expected to be when it is all over, it is important to talk about journey versus destiny. There is a vast difference between the two, and you cannot use one to judge the other, either at the beginning, or at the end. For example, a good comparison of journey versus destiny can be paralleled with the process of mining and processing gold. It is a long, tedious, sometimes dangerous process. It is fair to say that everyone likes one or more of these finished products, whether it is gold, silver, precious stones, marble, pearls, diamonds, you name it. However, there can be no finished product where there is not a process, and process is the hardest, longest, most challenging, and difficult. One therefore can conclude that in real life, nothing just happens! There is the saying, if it comes easy, it worth little or nothing. Enjoying the finished product does not give one an idea what it takes to produce it. Imagination without experience is not a trusted description, or a reliable testimony.

The same is true of a journey to any location whether you walk, ride, drive, fly or sail. Roads develop potholes, dangerous corners, hills up and down, detours and more: and if not properly navigated, it can result in serious harm, death, and dismemberment. Flights often have delays; bad weather, air-pocket: (a condition of the atmosphere that causes an airplane to drop suddenly) dangerous clouds that could cause a rough nerve shattering ride; we have heard of "bird strike" that blow holes in airplanes, or even affect the functionality of engines. Sailing can be badly affected with storm and winds that will cause even large vessels to become unstable, and be tossed to and fro on the waves of the sea. The point is, no one can guarantee what will happen on a journey once you get started. Even with a familiar route, things can change on a dime on any given day.

Therefore, when you get to your intended destiny, one cannot assume that because you got there the journey was easy. It is not possible, then, to tell what one has been through, in order to get to a certain place in their lives, nor can one understand the struggles; or the ups and downs, unless one has been there with him. That's one of the reasons one should not become envious of another's achievements. One never knows what it cost for you to get where you are. The third stanza of the great hymn, "There Were Ninety and Nine", written by Elizabeth Cecilia Clephane, says, "But none of the ransomed ever knew, how deep were the waters crossed; nor how dark was the night when the Lord passed thro' ere he found his sheep that was lost…" This song implies that end results never give the full picture of what it takes to get there. Sometimes it takes blood, sweat, and tears, determination and will combined together to make it to your destiny. On the other hand, you should never assume prematurely that because your journey is difficult, because your road is rough; because you have to struggle; because you stumble and even fall sometimes, you are not going to make it to your destiny. If you can separate the two, (journey versus destiny) you will be able to stay focused, and keep fighting even in the face of adversity. One of, if not my favorite quote is from an unknown author, which says, "The greatness of man is not what it takes to get him started, but what it takes to stop him". One of the downfalls of the Hebrew children as they journeyed from Egypt to the promise land, was that they lost focus of their promised destiny given to Moses by God himself. So they became discombobulated when things weren't going as they preconceived in their minds, and therefore they developed irrational behavior, and a rebellious attitude.

They had been in slavery for over four hundred years, and were happy to get out of Egypt at the word of Moses, (with all the miracles they saw, orchestrated by the hand of the I AM that I AM, the God of Abraham, Isaac, and Jacob who would take them to a land filled with milk and honey), but it was not long before they began to complain as they faced challenges on the journey. When they realized that it wasn't going to be easy, they started to complain. They soon forgot the promises of God that he, with his mighty hand, would get them to their destiny. As the journey began to get difficult and uncertain, especially realizing that Pharaoh had changed his mind on letting them go freely, they soon became frustrated, anxious, and began to complain.

Here is one thing to hold on to without wavering, when the Lord makes a promise, (unlike you and me who often has to figure it our along the way) he already foreknow what the obstacles would be every step of the way, and has pre-planned his strategies in order to bring the plan to actualization. Faith will become sight, but you must trust him. God promised that the glory would return to the temple, and the glory of the latter would be greater than the former, and by his mighty hand nothing seen, or unseen, could prevent it from happening. Solomon's temple was known for all its architectural marvel and splendor, something like which has never been seen before. As recorded in 1 Kings 6-8, it was an amazing wonder like which the world has never seen. All the vessels of the Lord along with many other artifacts; including the Ark of the Covenant was brought out of the city of David and was placed in the temple, in the most holy place. The priests, after placing the ark in its place following the sacrifices, the glory of the Lord filled the temple so that the priests could not minister. "And it came to pass, when the priests were come out of the holy place, that the cloud filled the house of the Lord, so that the priests could not minister because of the cloud: for the glory of the Lord had filled the house of the Lord. Then spake Solomon, the Lord said he would dwell in the thick darkness. I have surely build thee an house to dwell in, a settled place for thee to abide for ever" (1 Kings 8:10-13).

But about 587 BC, there was a siege on Jerusalem, and the great temple was eventually destroyed. You can only imagine the devastation it caused in the lives of the people, and how it affected their morale. Their hopes and pride crumbled with the loss of the temple. It was bad enough for the city to be sieged, but to have lost Solomon's temple, was cataclysmic. The place where they saw the glory of God so manifestly displayed that the priests could not minister; Solomon declaring that he had built a place for the Lord to abide in forever, and to see its destruction was nothing less than horrifying, they were terrified. Unlike Solomon however, the Lord knew all that would unfold before it happened, but he's never without a plan for his people, and he can never be caught off guard. God will not leave himself without glory, so whatever it takes to have his glory returns, he will do it. His glory he will not give to another, and he cannot be deprived of it, even if the rocks will have to cry out. So the Lord promised that the temple would be rebuilt, the glory shall return, and one of the most interesting things during this episode, was, he promised that the glory of the latter will be greater than the former. It was incomprehensible in the minds of those who knew Solomon's temple, to imagine that there could be a latter glory that would supersede the former. What they had in mind was only what they saw, and heard.

As recorded in Haggai 2:7-9, "And I will shake all nations, and the desire of all nations shall come: and I will fill this house with glory, saith the Lord of hosts. The silver is mine, and the gold is mine, saith the Lord of hosts. The glory of this latter house shall be greater than the former, saith the Lord of hosts: and in this place will I give peace, saith the Lord of hosts". Those who can only look back at what was—will have difficulties grasping what can, and will be. It is common human nature to become nostalgic. Zerubbabel and Jeshua, the remnant of their brethren and the priests and Levites—and many others who made it out of captivity back to Jerusalem, appointed young men from twenty years and older to do the construction of the new temple, they converge on the project with enthusiasm. "And when the builders laid the foundation of the temple of the Lord, they set the priests in their apparel with trumpets, and the Levites the sons of Asaph with cymbals, to praise the Lord after the ordinance of David the king of Israel" (Ezra 3:10). The people sang and shouted praise together unto the Lord for his goodness and mercy endures forever towards Israel. However, not everyone was looking forward jubilantly, anticipating the completion and the latter glory. Many of the priests, Levites, and chief of the fathers, who were "ancient men", (according to Ezra), men who were familiar with the former house, they did not play cymbals and shout as they saw the foundations of the new temple erected before their eyes. Instead, they wept with a loud voice, while others were shouting aloud for joy. Both groups were of equal intensity, so that the onlookers, or the distant listeners could not differentiate between the shout for joy of the jubilant, or the sound of weeping by the distressed. The weepers got stuck mentally and emotionally with what was familiar to them. It was so deeply engrained in their psyche that they couldn't break through the barrios of their minds.

Nostalgia holds you gripped to the past, and obscures the future. This truth was evident in the behavior of these ancient men, locked into history, and totally withdrawn from the future, even at the Lord's declaration that the latter glory will be greater than the former.

The glory of God is often described or presented in the form of a cloud, and a cloud generally provides a covering. Clouds in Scripture are used for various cultural, traditional, or epiphanic reasons. Sometimes negative, but often positive: for judgment, for rain, for blessings, and for God's presence... So then, what is important is the context in which the reference has been made. The Hebrew word (aw-nawn) refers to covering the sky... It also speaks of a cloud mass of Theophanic proportion—which is the visible manifestation of deity.

One may wonder why were there so many instances in the Scriptures that we see God's presence described as cloud, or within the clouds? Cloud suggests, or implies, that the presence of the Lord is here. It seems likewise that it is designed to breakdown the intensity of the glory of God to the level where mortal man would not be consumed by his presence. You and I know that the only time you can take a full look at the sun without serious effect on the eyes is when there is a cloud cover, or the use of manmade protection for the eyes from the ray of the sun. Before one can have a conversation about the Glory returning to the Temple/House, one must first acknowledge this, for something to return it means it was once there. If there is a need for it to return, it means it is no longer there because it has left, or has been taken away. Ezekiel saw the glory of the Lord leave Jerusalem via the eastern side of the city, because that's where God came from... The east is where the ultimate force of wind or power comes from. When God was ready to part the red sea, he caused an east wind to blow all night. The Hebrew and Greek words refer to wind, also refers to breath, life, and Spirit. Just an added note according to Merrill F. Unger in his 1985 Dictionary of the Bible, "The east wind crosses the sandy wastes of Arabia Deserta before reaching Palestine, and was hence termed 'the wind of the wilderness' (Job 1:19; Jer. 13:24). It blows with violence, and is hence supposed to be used generally for a violent wind". The glory of the Lord manifested in the cloud in the Old Testament, is manifested by the move of the Holy Spirit in the church.

There is something interesting that happened as recorded in Ezekiel 11:22, "And the glory of the Lord went up from the midst of the city and stood upon the mountain which is on the east side of the city". It departed from the midst, but it did not disappear, it remained in sight. Apparently it stayed right on the Mount of Olives waiting to return as soon as Israel was willing to repent and turn from their transgressions and backsliding. If there is one thing that can be said about God, is that he has proven himself loyal to his people, and likewise to his church. Even if he had to chasten, rebuke, or chastise, he turns around and give people the option to turn around from doing the wrong, and he will turn also and restore his relationship with them. God is always waiting for us to make the adjustment and repent. Just like his arms are waiting to welcome his repentant child, the imminent return of his glory is just hanging over his house, waiting to return. If the glory of the Lord is not in the temple, it's nothing more than a building occupied by human beings. If the Spirit of God is not operational in the church, it's nothing more than a social gathering of opinionated people vying to have their voices heard, and that leaves little to convince the world of the power and majesty of God. Let it be known, that amidst the noise, amidst the distractions, amidst the perceptions, amidst the lamentation and nostalgia about what used to be, God will not walk away from his house, he may withdraw temporarily in order to create the awareness of our helplessness without him, but he is always just a breadth away waiting for his people to humble themselves, pray, and seek his face. It is clearly recorded in the Chronicles, "If my people, which are called by my name, shall humble themselves, and pray, and seek my face, and turn from their wicked ways; then will I hear from heaven, and forgive their sin, and will heal their land"(2 Chronicles 7:14). This is also proof that God is never willing to part with his people even when they have sinned. We see that as God's deliberate act in the Old Testament, and continued even more by the sacrifice of Christ on the cross. The things that were written aforetime were written for our learning. So to get an understanding of how God will deal with his people in the age of the church, it is important to look back at his dealing with his chosen people during the Old Testament age of the law. What is there to learn? We learn that he promises to be with his children in good times and bad times. That does not mean however, that he overlooks and accepts transgressions or rebelliousness, or, that sin will go unpunished. Nevertheless, every one who repents will receive God's forgiveness. David attests to that, that a broken and contrite heart God will not despise.

Later in another vision Ezekiel writes in chapter 43, "Afterward he brought me to the gate, even the gate that looketh toward the east: and, behold the glory of the God of Israel came from the way of the east: and his voice was like a noise of many water: and the earth shined with his glory…And the glory of the Lord came into the house by the way of the gate whose prospect is toward the east. So the spirit took me up, and brought me into the inner court; and, behold, the glory of the Lord filled the house". (Ezekiel 43:1-5). This we know has Messianic prophetic implications, but it also tells us that no matter what, the glory will return to the house. The only contingency is our willingness to repent and turn to the Lord.

The church (in the eyes of many) may be going through a moment of transition, it may appear that the glory has been removed, but one thing that we should not lose sight of, and is that Christ promised to present it to himself, a glorious church. The example the Apostle Paul used projecting how a man should love his wife in the same way Christ loves the church. "Husbands, love your wives, even as Christ loved the church, and gave himself for it; that he might sanctify and cleanse it with the washing of water by the word, that he might present it to himself a glorious church, not having spot, or wrinkle, or any such thing; but that it should be holy and without blemish" (Ephesians 5:25-28). The emphasis here is that Christ will present the church, his bride, to himself a glorious (a glory that is splendid, noble, gorgeous and honorable) church…" That adjective "glorious" describes in a broad sense what the status of the church will be when Christ receives it. That word (en'-dox-os) means to be splendid, to be held in great esteem, and of high repute. When it comes to God's plan for his church nothing present or future can alter his plan. No person or persons, principalities or powers will be able to derail what God had put in place.

For those who live in reminiscence of what the church used to be, and not what it will be, (like the ancient men in the days of Zerubbabel who only wept over Solomon's temple remembering what it was, but not what God said the new one would be) bear this one thing in mind, Jesus told Peter that he would build his church, and the gates of hell will not prevail against it. While I am not suggesting that we become reckless, lackadaisical, or incontinent and allow the flesh to dominate our lives so that we fall into an apostate position we must be reminded that the church belongs to Christ, and he promised to present it to himself a glorious church. Interesting that he will be presenting her, his bride, to himself. It is not the norm that a groom prepares his bride for himself, the groom awaits to see what his bride looks like when she arrives for their wedding day. The most glorious time of a woman's life is normally her wedding day. Extra effort is made to make sure she appears looking her best. Maybe the only time she needs helping hands to make her ready for what is considered a once in a lifetime moment. The groom waits to see how she will appear to charm his heart. Unlike Christ, he knows ahead of time what his bride will look like. Christ will not be waiting for chance to determine how his bride will appear. He will not be depending on some Bishop, Priest, Pastor, or any designated person to determine how, when, and under what condition she will be ready, He will prepare her for himself.

In every generation and dispensation, man, who lives in the fallen nature of Adam, fails at all points. It is not hard to see why Christ holds on to the headship of the church. Yes he has given gifts, talents, ministries that will help in preparing the church, but ultimately he has the last say. It is not known how or when Christ will come for his church, but one thing is known, it will not be a puny church struggling to survive at the mercy of some scrupulous or unscrupulous people prone to make mistakes, or lapse in judgment. Every now and then you can hear the resounding echoes of lamentation over the church and its current status. There is one final glory, and if it is not there now keep holding on, the glory will return! The latter days of the church will be brighter and greater than it has ever been. For those who are concerned about its future whether it will be bright, dormant, or effective… whether it has lost its power, or will soar in the last days, keep the faith and continue to push forward. It remains the church of Jesus Christ, and he remains the head of it. The Apostle Paul reminds us of the foundation that it is built on. One, Jesus told Peter at the time of the great revelation concerning who he (Christ) was, and the establishing of his (Christ's) ecclesia (church) that he will build his church, and the gates of hell shall not prevail against it. The church is not left to the mercy of this moment of changing culture, the variableness of doctrinal beliefs, or man's tradition. Jesus compares the church to his body, and he made it clear that he is the head. There is an irrefutable reason that he is the head of his church and not us, not matter what position one may hold. Here is the truth—a man can live without almost any member of his body except his head. The foundation of the church is built on the apostles and prophets, but Jesus Christ himself is the chief corner stone.

Everyone must work out his salvation with fear and trembling. One can drop out of the church, corrupt himself—cause havoc in his corner, destroy the lives of some, negatively impact or influence the lives of others, but that will not, and cannot destroy the body of Christ. God in his eternal wisdom and power would never leave the church's destiny to be determined by mortal man who has always failed. To borrow a few verses from Joel 2 in his promise of restoration he says, "Be glad then, ye children of Zion, and rejoice in the Lord your God: for he hath given you the former rain moderately, and he will cause to come down for you the rain, the former rain and the latter rain in the first month. And the floors shall be full of wheat, and the fats shall overflow with wine and oil. And I will restore to you the years that the locust hath eaten, the cankerworm, and the caterpillar, and the palmerworm, my great army which I sent among you. And ye shall eat plenty, and be satisfied, and praise the name of the Lord your God, that hath dealt wondrously with you: and my people shall never be ashamed" (Joel 2:23-26). The character of God has been demonstrated throughout history in no uncertain manner—how he has redeemed his people out of captivity, rebuild his temple, and cause his glory to return. The same has been true of the church as she rose from suppression and oppression; she rose out of the dark ages, and it will be true of her in the final lap for home. This is authenticated by Joel, (Ch. 2:28-29) and confirmed by Peter at Pentecost in Acts 2. The skeptics and ignorant onlookers at Pentecost had no knowledge of what they were seeing by the outpouring of the Holy Spirit on those who waited at Jerusalem. They'd never seen such operation except among the drunken, but Peter standing up, influenced by the anointing and unction of the Holy Spirit that he had just been a recipient of: speaking with power, authority and conviction declared, "For these are not drunken as ye suppose, seeing it is but the third hour of the day. (9 o'clock in the morning) But this is that which was spoken by the prophet Joel; and it shall come to pass in the last days, saith God, I will pour out of my Spirit upon all flesh: and your sons and your daughters shall prophesy, and your young men shall see visions, and your old men shall dream dreams: and on my servants and on my handmaidens I will pour out in those days of my Spirit; and they shall prophesy" (Acts 2:15-18).

    The Jews then would have understood that Joel's declaration was a Messianic prophecy; hence an understanding of its fulfillment confirming that the Messiah had come. As Peter continued to preach and reminded them of the rejection, and crucifixion of Christ, and how God had raised him up they were pricked in their hearts and asked what they should do. They were admonished by Peter to repent, and be baptized every one of them in the name of Jesus for the remission of their sins, and they too would become eligible to receive the gift of the Holy Ghost. Jesus told his disciples it was expedient for them that he go back to his Father, because that would clear the way for the Holy Ghost to come. One of the important reasons for the coming of the Holy Spirit was that his job description would be broader than that of Christ's limited time on earth, moving around in human form. Yes he is always God, but in human flesh he subjected himself to the limitations of being only at one place at a time. The Holy Spirit who would not simply dwell among the disciples, (unlike the Ark of the Covenant that dwelled among the people) he would indwell them, which means wherever they go, he goes. Christ himself in the gospel of John told his disciples, "Nevertheless I tell you the truth; It is expedient for you that I go away: for if I go not away, the Comforter will not come unto you; but if I depart, I will send him unto you. And when he is come, he will reprove the world of sin, and of righteousness, and of judgment: of sin, because they believe not on me; of righteousness, because I go to my Father, and ye see me no more; of judgment, because the prince of this world is judged" (John 16:7-11). In John 14:26 they were told, "But when the Comforter, which is the Holy Ghost, whom the Father will send in my name, he shall teach you all things, and bring all things to your remembrance, whatsoever I have said unto you". This is an indication of the vastness of the ministry, ability, and operation of the Holy Spirit. That means he has been the one influencing the work and operation of the church ever since Pentecost, because Christ had already left ten days prior. On his last day on earth, at the time leading up to his ascension, his last words to the disciples were, "But ye shall receive power, after that the Holy Ghost is come upon you; and ye shall be witnesses unto me both in Jerusalem, (which is considered home) and in Judea, (considered next door) and in Samaria, (considered the abandoned and rejected places), and unto the uttermost parts of the earth" (Acts 1:8). The glory shall return to the last days' church, no matter how it looks in the eyes of the onlookers. Under the watchful oversight of the Holy Spirit, with the attributes and power as the third person in the Godhead, he will prepare the church for her glorious presentation to Christ. The wheat and the tears will grow together until the day of harvest. There are many who are concerned, worried, and confused about what they see happening in churches in their local areas, or what they see on television. However, it is not new, Jesus gave a great example of the mystery parable of the wheat and tears in Matthew 13:24-30.

The disciples' comportment was not within the guidelines Jesus gave them. It falls in line with the mentality you see in the church today. There are those who believe that they are the fixers, the husbandmen, the sifter, or the ones who can purge the church, or root up the tears in order to make the church perfect. This is exactly one of the reasons Christ gave the parable. Read Matthew 13:24-30, and you will see the parable of the kingdom like a man who sowed good seed in his field, and the enemy sowed tares while they slept. The servants saw that tares were among the wheat, and enquired of the householder trying to find out how that had happened, he told them it was done by the enemy, and they aptly were ready to get to work to root up the tares. The logic behind the parable is that, in an effort to remove the tares from among the wheat at the time they wanted, would pose great danger to the harvest. However, at harvest time, it will be clear, and easier to identify wheat from tares. At harvest, the tares will be removed first, and burned, and the wheat will be gathered into the barn. For those who cannot see the glory of the church, keep looking, and if you can't see clearly, trust the Lord of the harvest, he figured it out before time began. Christ alone is worthy to cleanse, and make his church ready to present to his Father, and it will be glorious without blemish, without spots or wrinkles, or any such things. The struggles are not new; the so called dull moments of uncertainty are not unfamiliar to the body of Christ, but her eternal destiny has been sealed ever since Christ established it while he was on earth. The gates of hell shall not prevail over the church no matter where the attacks are coming from. It was clear in the mind of Christ that it would not be without attacks from principalities and powers, but within the presence and influence of the Holy Spirit, the powers of darkness will not prevail.

What is important as we enter into these times of uncertainties, everyone who names the name of the Lord ought to make the pursuit of righteousness their top priority. Especially in this age of the expansion of social media, and the bombardment of unsolicited graphics and popup messages, the children of God must guard the loins of the mind as the devil ramps up the pressure, and intensifies the attacks on our core values, moral, and spiritual tenets we hold dear. The tenacity of the believer seeking after righteousness must rise to the same level and beyond that of the enemy, remembering that greater is he that is within us than he that is in the world. Just like going to a gunfight with a knife would be virtually suicidal, we cannot casually face the enemy of our souls unprepared to fight and push back at anything he throws at us. Not being prepared for the battle we are in is being prepared to lose the fight. We are in a spiritual warfare, and in this battle we must fight fire with fire. The fiery darts of the wicked can only be quenched by the power and fire of the Holy Spirit. Therefore, we must be building a spiritual house. Nothing less will be able to stand against the principalities and powers, the rulers of the darkness of this world, and the spiritual wickedness we see even in high places. As the church fights and wins, it will become a beacon to the world, and will generate hope to the hopeless. Peter started off his epistle by thanking God for his abundant mercy that had begotten them again unto a lively hope. This hope of living again has been influenced by the resurrection of Christ. This inheritance incorruptible and undefiled fades not away, and is reserved in heaven for you, but one should not believe that it comes easily, or automatically. He informed them how they are kept by faith, and although they may have had seasonal heaviness through manifold temptations, but their trials will turn into praise at the appearing of Jesus Christ. In Chapter 4:10 he tells them of the manifold grace of God. He told them to gird up the loins of their minds and be sober, he reminds them of the holiness of Christ, and it was also required of them likewise to be holy. They were not redeemed with corruptible things like silver and gold, but with the precious and efficacious blood of Christ the lamb without blemish. He reminded them that everything fades away leaving only God's word that will endure forever. What is going to hold us together in the midst of this intense battle, give us the strength and ammunition adequate for this unconventional war, and keep the church from falling? It is the word of God! What will sanctify and keep us unspotted and uncontaminated from the pollutions of the world? It is the word of God! How will one be able to cleanse his ways, it's by taking heed to the word of God. "Thy word have I hid in my heart, that I might not sin against thee"(Psalm 119:11).

THE WORD IN MY HEART

The overarching goal of every believer ought to be, (without exception), a deep-rooted desire for hiding God's word in our hearts. Without the word of God hidden in our hearts at this crucial juncture in the life of the church, it will have adverse effect on our ability to resist the devil, and put us in danger of being sucked up by external influence. It would be like an automobile driving down the street without engine oil. Everything appears ok until the combustion chamber overheats, and if not shut down for immediate attention, it will begin to burn and melt the rings and pistons, and eventually cause the engine to seize. Without the fullness of the Spirit of God in the life of the Christian it is like a vehicle driving down the street that is dependent on fuel to feed the acceleration system in order to keep driving to your destiny but realize the tank is empty. So then, because we cannot fight, survive, understand the promises of God, know how to live a life of sanctification and walk in righteousness without the guidance of the word of God, and influence of the Spirit, it is incumbent on us to spare no cost in getting a good hold on what thus saith the Lord. Sometimes we browse pass the depth of what the word implies, casually reading a Psalm as a custom or out of necessities: so take a little deeper look at what the inspired writer wrote in this Psalm.

The word he used to express his inner desires for protecting the word of God in order to retain their benefits, is the word "hid". That word is a primitive root word that means to hide by covering; it means to protect; or to keep in a secret place. That means, he intended to take deliberate action to secure and protect God's word not on manuscripts, or scrolls, but in his heart. Note also where he intentionally wants to have the word kept, in his heart and not in his head. There are many who can tell you what the word says from great memory, but the word has no positive impact on their hearts. The expression says, locked up in the deep of my heart O Lord, are your words, and I will draw from it as it becomes necessary to lift my faith. I will draw from them when I am discouraged; I will draw strength from them when I am weak; I will turn to them when I need direction. When the flesh wants to drag me down the wrong path, I will turn to them. When the waters of life are overflowing me, I will find refuge in them. When the sand is shifting under my feet, I will find in them a rock to stand on. I will hide them in my heart not for their safety, because they are forever settled in heaven. I will hide them in my heart so that they will keep me from falling, and prevent me from sinning against thee.

The devil keeps going around like a vulture looking for something to devour, and if the word of God is not hidden in the heart of the believer, he will soon realize that the enemy will snap it away little by little. If you doubt that truth turn to what Jesus told his disciples as he gave them the interpretation to the parable in Matthew 13:18-23 "Hear ye therefore the parable of the sower. When anyone hears the word of the kingdom, and understands it not, then cometh the wicked one, and catch away that which was in his heart. This is he which receive seed by the wayside... But he that receive seeds into good ground is he that hear the word, and understands it: which also bears fruit, and brings forth fruit, some a hundred, some sixty, and some thirty". So here he made mention of the word falling by the wayside and picked up by the fowls of the air. That explicitly states that when the word is not hidden it becomes exposed to the enemy who wants to snatch it away. Don't ever underestimate the fact that the devil knows the importance of the word in the life of a child of God. He knows they are lamp to your feet and light to your path. He knows that God's word will bring you comfort in your lonely moments. He knows that God's word in your heart gives you hope in your time of despair, and he is terrified anytime he sees you making good of, and digesting it.

We are endeavoring to build a spiritual house, and it will not have a solid foundation without the knowledge of, and application of God's words in our hearts.

Those who are born of the Spirit ought to do one thing, and it is to build a spiritual house. You are not born of the flesh—that was then, (born of your mother and father) that which is born of the flesh is flesh. This is now! You are born of the Spirit incorruptible, and therefore must bring forth spiritual fruit.

WE ARE BUILDING A SPIRITUAL HOUSE

Here is how you pursue that! The first thing is to develop an earnest desire for spiritual growth, by seeking to understand the fundamentals of Christian faith; constant indulgence in prayer and fasting, and daily meditation. In general, to develop a healthy immune system for a baby, nothing is more important than the mother's milk.

The apostle says, as newborn babes desiring the sincere milk of the word that you may grow thereby. The word "desire" (ep-ee-poth-eh-o) means to dote upon, i.e. intensely crave possession, to desire greatly. The desire for knowing God's word is one of the high points of fast growth and spiritual maturity. Let's take our cue from Christ who coming as unto a living stone, disallowed of men, but chosen of God and precious. As lively stones, our responsibility is to build a spiritual house. The stone by itself has little value and beauty, but in the house its full beauty is seen and appreciated. Let's all buckle up and build together like Nehemiah and his people in the rebuilding of Jerusalem. There is great danger in trying to do our own thing separately. The devil is quite afraid when the church moves and builds together. As individuals we become a target, but together we are a force to deal with. CHRIST IS BUILDING A SPIRITUAL HOUSE… but not every, and any material can be used in building God's spiritual house. Dead stones build fleshly house, lively stones build spiritual house…there are two builders, and you know their houses by the material they use to build.

In Galatians 5 we see some of the things that will build or destroy a spiritual house, and they are called the works of the flesh, and the fruit of the Spirit. "Now the works of the flesh are manifest, which are these; Adultery, fornication, uncleanness, lasciviousness, Idolatry, witchcraft, hatred, variance, emulations, wrath, strife, seditions, heresies, Envyings, murders, drunkenness, revellings, and such like: of the which I tell you before, as I have also told you in time past, that they which do such things shall not inherit the kingdom of God". (Those are the destructive elements of the flesh that inevitably prevents one from being spiritual, and therefore unable to build a spiritual house. However, here are the pieces of the fruit of the Spirit with will without a doubt, build a spiritual house). "But the fruit of the Spirit is love, joy, peace, longsuffering, gentleness, goodness, faith, Meekness, temperance: against such there is no law. And they that are Christ's have crucified the flesh with the affections and lusts"(Galatians 5:19-22).

Because we are building a spiritual house, God's Shekinah Glory will return in the last days, and the world will see the full manifestation of the Son of God as he comes back to take his church out of this troubled world. The clouds are again gathering, and that means, it is about to rain the latter rain.

Where there is no cloud there is no rain… When the cloud is heavy there is a chance of rain; where there is **OMINOUS** cloud there is **IMMINENT** rain, so position yourself, and get your vessels ready, there is going to be torrential rain until we are spiritually saturated. Just make sure when the rain begins to fall you are strategically positioned for it to fall on you. This is not over by a long shot, Christ is getting ready for the Father to give the go ahead for his church, and she will be shining garments pure and spotless, ready for the marriage supper of the lamb. Don't be left behind, and don't be caught up in the fallacies of the day, and get distracted from what it most important. Don't allow yourself to be influenced with erroneous doctrines of devils, and miss your moment to be ready for the rapture. One does not have to believe, or accept truth in order to make it truth. No one believed that the floods would come during Noah's time because of the nonsensical building of a large boat in the desert. That's what makes God, God, because he does the unthinkable, and the things of God, are foolishness with man, until he sees it with his own eyes. BE READY!

CONCLUSION

These seven churches mentioned in Revelation 2–3 are significant to the life of the church of Christ on earth, and their references should never be taken slightly. There are many views, however, concerning whether they were specifically designed by Christ as examples of the churches throughout the dispensation. Some believe they bare no relations to the church as it is today, rather they are some historic story that should not make its way as relatively significant, or applicable to the church as it is today. Others, on the other hand, believe these churches were symbols of what the church would look like and the things it would experience through temptations, trials, persecution, and martyrdom. Therefore, the lessons learned from Christ's letters should not be slighted and overlooked.

Throughout the history of God dealing with his people, he often used examples to demonstrate his power, such as bringing the

Hebrew children out of Egyptian bondage with a "strong hand" as the Scripture often mentions.

> And it shall be for a sign unto thee upon thine hand, and for a memorial between thine eyes, that the Lord's law may be in thy mouth: for with a strong hand hath the Lord brought thee out of Egypt. Thou shalt therefore keep this ordinance in his season from year to year. (Exodus 13:9–10)

There are many examples of backsliding and restoration that God used in the Bible to confirm to or inform his people that he will always have his hands open to the penitent heart that repents and returns to him. It is said, that if there is one thing God cannot do, is turn his back on a broken and contrite heart.

As one continues to observe the Scripture, he will undoubtedly realize that there are examples of rebellion and the consequences that followed, especially when it comes to the people of God coming out of Egypt, on their way to the promised land, and thereafter. The apostle Paul said, "For whatsoever things were written aforetime were written for our learning, that we through patience and comfort of the Scriptures might have hope" (Romans 15:4). As a matter of fact, there are examples of life experiences, (good or bad) for all to learn from and understand God's dealings with his people.

It should be safe to say that all pastors and leaders, including laymen, should learn from the characteristics and examples of these churches to avoid falling into the same trap as those who fell from grace. Like any church today, these churches had their strengths and weaknesses. Still, two of them were not found to have done any wrong, however, they were still mentioned as examples for us, and lessons to learn from. They suffered at the hands of the Enemy, and they were not rebuked by Christ because they had behaved themselves wisely under pressure and persecution, and exhibited great grace in the face of adversity.

On the other hand, there were those that could not resist the temptation of the flesh and the influence of the world, so they got caught in the trap of gratifying the flesh.

> Many have attempted to make sense of Revelation chapters 2 and 3 (the letters to the seven churches of Asia) by taking them as a unified whole. It is significant that Jesus chose these particular seven congregations to address, though there were other churches in the region which were not written to (such as the church at Collosse). Additionally, some have pointed to the order of the letters as evidence of their significance as a broad explanation of church history in the period between the Ascension and Jesus to His return.
>
> It is also interesting to note that Paul addressed seven churches: Rome, Corinth, Galatia, Ephesus, Collosse, Phillipi, and Thessalonica (some also note with interest that Jesus gives seven "Kingdom Parables"). Early commentators on the Book of Revelation emphasized that as seven is a number of completion and fulfillment, so Jesus and Paul wrote to seven churches as an indication that they were in fact speaking to the complete church, not just these seven congregations. Speaking to seven churches means speaking to the church in perfection, in completion and totality. As one commentator puts it, "The churches of all time are comprehended in seven."[164]

The church of Ephesus, well known as the church that left its first love, was a hardworking church. It was patient but had little tolerance for those who were bent on doing evil. It scrutinized and evaluated all

---

164 David Guzik, Rev., 3.

those who said they were apostles and found them liars. It had keen discernment when it came to others but was completely oblivious to its own emptiness. That is nothing far from what you will see today among individuals. It is so easy to point out the wrongs of others while leaving their own wrongs unattended. It left its first love, suggesting that it deliberately did so. There is a difference in leaving something and losing it. This church did not lose their love, but they left it, which suggests they would be able to find it. Hence, Christ's admonition to them to remember from whence they had fallen and repent and be restored or have their candlestick removed. The devil can't take away your love for Christ, but he can frustrate you and cause you to walk away, because man will always have free will. However, he should never forget to calculate the consequences of walking away from expressing his love for Christ. They hated the evil deeds of the Nicolaitans as Christ did, but their fellowship was under false pretenses. It makes no sense to curse the devil if you do not genuinely embrace fellowship with Christ. It is of little worth to curse the darkness when you refuse to shine your own light.

This church typifies an individual or group that is only about outward action and has no intimacy with Christ. Paul describes this as "having a form of godliness, but denying the power thereof" (2 Timothy 3:5). The church today must be aware that if its love for Christ has gone cold or is nonexistent, words or actions are not an acceptable substitute to the Lord. The truth is that God and Christ will accept no substitute for any principle, law, or statute that they have established as guidelines for all to follow.

The church of Smyrna, the persecuted church, had been through tremendous tribulation with little resources. As a result, it was labeled as being in poverty. It was abused, tortured, and martyred for its testimony of faith in Christ. Though it had little to live on, it was rich in faith and would not allow external forces, physical needs, or social estrangement to cause it to sin against the God it loved.

The church of Smyrna was the total opposite of the Laodicean church that thought it needed nothing but was naked, poor, blind, and miserable. This church was rich with little material gain. Christ introduced himself to them as he that was dead and is alive to give them hope. Those who had died for their faith would be alive again just as he was. And those who would yet face persecution and even death were to be courageous and use him as their example. Death for the cause of Christ was not a loss, it would be great gain as Paul reminded us. "For to me to live is Christ, and to die is gain"(Philippians 1:21).

The people of the church of Smyrna lived in a prosperous city but were not the benefactors of the wealth, because they would not compromise their faith or commitment to Christ, in order to change their socioeconomic lifestyle. They valued their status in Christ over material gain and social status. They lived among pretenders who were religiously driven but not relationally loyal to Christ. They were among those who were of the synagogue of Satan, pretending to be who they were not. They were admonished by Christ to stand strong in the face of adversity and hold onto their faith. A great part of this church's persecution was because it blatantly refused to burn a bit of incense and state that Caesar was Lord. As a result, they were considered outlaws, which intensified their persecution.

> They would not give to no man the name of Lord; that name they would keep for Jesus Christ and Jesus Christ alone. They would not even formally conform. Uncompromisingly the Christians refused to go through the form of Caesar worship, and therefore the Christians were outlaws and liable to persecution at any time.[165]

---

165 William Barclay, 19.

They were like the Hebrew boys who refused to bow to the king for fear of death. It was more important to stick to the principles they were brought up with whether they lived or die. So it was made clear to Nebuchadnezzar that the God of their fathers whom they served would deliver them, and even if for whatever reason he chose not to deliver them, still they refuse to bow or worship his images. The Smyrna church lived constantly under the threat of death, but refuse to capitulate. It seems that they never knew what would happen next, but Christ's encouragement must have brought them a sense of relief and hope: "Fear none of those things which thou shalt suffer; behold, the devil shall cast some of you into prison, that ye may be tried; and ye shall have tribulation ten days: Be thou faithful unto death; and I will give thee the crown of life" (Revelation 2:10). Whether this referenced ten literal days, which was unlikely, or ten years, which some commentators believe, or over a period of ten Roman emperors as other commentators believe, the most significant things to observe is that Christ placed a timeline on what the suffering would be like, and he gave them a time period. "Nowhere can life have been more dangerous for Christians than in Smyrna. As far back as 196 B.C. Smyrna had been the first in the world to erect a temple to Dea Roma, the goddess Rome."[166] This church could rest assured of the promises of God because he who is faithful had promised. Peter says, think is not strange concerning the fiery trials that come to try you, though some strange things happen to you. Strange things have happened, and stranger things will happen, but God will not allow you to be tempted above what you will be able to bear, and he will with those trials and temptations provide a way to escape.

The first thought from Jesus to the church of Pergamos was that he hath the sharp sword, indicating the power or sharpness of the Word or God. He was ready for them to know that his words in his

---

166 Ibid.

letter would be cutting like a two-edged sword because his rebuke was very strong, and there were many things for them to be aware of.

They were dwelling where Satan's house was, as Jesus noted. They were trying to have it both ways. The province or city of Pergamos was a stronghold of satanic forces and power, which made it even more challenging for the church, but God has always provided needed grace for his children to make it through all adversity, even if they died for his cause. He told his disciples, "And fear not them which kill the body, but are not able to kill the soul: but rather fear him which is able to destroy both soul and body in hell" (Matthew 10:28).

They did not deny his name, but they did all the wrong things while holding fast to their faith and testimony of Christ. Christ recognized his faithful Antipas, who had been martyred at the place where Satan dwelled. But even after all of that, there were a few things Christ had against them.

Although Christ said there were a few things, when they are observed, there were major problems, so it's no wonder Christ introduced himself as the one with the two-edged sword. Nothing cuts through a man's heart like the word of God, and it does so in the greatest disguise known only to the man who feels the impact. They had violated all the doctrinal principles they had been taught except not denying the name of Christ and holding onto their faith. Yes, it is hard to believe that they really held tight the name of Christ and the confession of faith while doing all the other wrong things. The classic irony we see in the church today. You can see with the naked eyes the hypocrisy of individuals and organizations pretending to be in fine fellowship with Christ, yet everything else in behavior and action says otherwise. A good example of how they could be compared is Christ's description of the scribes and Pharisees: "Woe unto you, scribes and Pharisees, hypocrites! For, ye are like unto whited sepulchers which indeed appear beautiful outward, but are within full of dead men's bones, and of all uncleanness" (Matthew 23:27).

There were those who held the doctrine of Balaam, which was symbolic to corrupt teachings of all sorts. One can remember the story of Balaam and Balak in Numbers 22–24. Balak wanted to curse Israel and Balaam bought into his bribery and caused God's intervention. This was the height of immorality and idol worship, as Balaam required that Balak build him seven altars and he offered on all of them. So under the doctrine of Balaam, one will find the doctrine of corruption. In the end, he taught Balak to cast a stumbling block before Israel, to eat things offered to idols and commit fornication.

Others among them held the doctrine of the Nicolaitans that taught sexual immorality. This doctrine stemmed from Nicolaus, a heretic, who believed and taught that it was okay to have a community of wives. Christ's blunt statement to this church was that he hated these things.

> These six things doth the Lord hate: yea, seven are an abomination unto him: A proud look, a lying tongue, and hands that shed innocent blood, An heart that deviseth wicked imaginations, feet that be swift in running to mischief, A false witness that speaketh lies, and he that soweth discord among brethren. (Proverbs 6:16–19)

This behavior was numbered among the abominable things that God abhors and warranted Christ's promise to fight against them with the sword of his mouth unless they repented.

The church of Thyatira, while it was located in the smallest and least important city of the seven churches, actually received the longest letter from Christ. Jesus' introduction to them was one of consuming fire and judgment. This is the only one of the churches that Christ twice told he knew of their works. He recognized their charity, patience, and faith, and then he mentioned their works.

This is important because, as he did with Pergamos, Christ had a few things against this church. Their last set of works had surpassed the first. They seemed to have accomplished more works in the latter times than they had previously. It is fascinating to imagine that a person or a church can practice two things and be known for them both. The church at Pergamos was acknowledged by Christ for its patience—charity, and faith. These are three very commendable and noteworthy things for any church. But their hypocrisy was astounding, for at the same time that they were charitable, patient, and practiced great faith, they were allowing Jezebel, who called herself a prophetess, to teach and seduce the people to commit fornication and to eat things offered to idols. This was not Ahab's wife mentioned in 1 Kings 18–19 but another woman with the same character. The name Jezebel is used as a synonym for an overbearing, nagging woman and also as a false teacher. With that said, some commentators believe that this may not have been a woman as a person, but rather a portrayal of the characteristics of the individual.

It is without doubt a dangerous thing for any church to give freedom and access to one who teaches false doctrine and who lives a life of immorality. This will destroy the church from within. Human nature by itself, even in a godly environment is prone to sin and wandering, so it is not surprising that Jezebel's teaching in the church of Thyatira would soon negatively impact some of the faithful brethren. That is a danger zone for any church to travel. It is happening today like it happened then. Some pastors and leaders are inclined to have certain people in their podium that they leave their congregants vulnerable to false teachings not having effectively vetted speakers and preachers before giving them the platform to speak freely. That is a dangerous thing to do because when some people are gone they leave a lot of mess behind to be cleaned up, and can cause disruption in your congregation. Jesus attested to that, declaring that Jezebel seduced his servants to commit adultery and to eat meat offered unto idols.

The opportunity and space was given to Jezebel to repent or face being cast onto a bed of sickness and affliction along with those who partook of her teachings. Again, here is God who is not quick to wrath, but plenteous in mercy, giving even the most notorious character the opportunity to stop and turn around. Christ promised to make an example of this group of Jezebel followers. "And I will kill her children with death: and all the churches shall know that I am he which searcheth the reigns and hearts: and I will give unto every one of you according to your works" (Revelation 2:23). It is a great thing to know that God does not use one man's work to judge another. He is faithful and just and will not give one what he has not earned (other than the gift of God's grace and love). The wisdom and justice of God goes beyond human comprehension. Every man will be judged and rewarded according to what he has done with his own body.

The church of Thyatira is typical of the church today with members who are bent toward their own ways. Many churches have cliques, based on ideological, philosophical, and doctrinal differences. There are some who believe you can do what you want with impunity and God will forgive, while others believe there are strict standards and statutes that God established and ought to be adhered to. Within this church clearly there was great divide, but in the end, God rewarded the faithful. God will never bundle you up for reward or punishment, because there are degrees of punishment, and categories of rewards. What you work for is what you will be rewarded for.

Another point of note here is that within any congregation, God can find individuals who have been faithful to his Word or the doctrine they have been taught and will reward them, not organizations. That is why you really cannot judge one because of where they worship, but how and why they do.

The church of Sardis had fallen asleep. It was a half dead church, as a portion of its members were dead and the rest were in danger of dying. This church had had many struggles as Jesus noted that he had not found their work perfect. It was living under the umbrella of what was. It had previously held a good name and reputation, but that was not what it was known for. Outwardly, it was known for good, but inwardly, it had fallen and was living under false pretenses.

This can be contrasted to many church organizations today. They are but a shadow of what they were twenty to thirty years ago. While it can be said and justified that many were overbearing with their legalistic views, organizational principles, and doctrines that had no biblical base, they made their names with a high standard of living. As a result, maybe out of fear of excommunication and lack of intimacy with Christ, their teachings were adhered to.

Many of these churches today are living on what was, a shadow of who they were, similar to the church of Sardis. However, the church of Sardis was commended for having heard the Word, holding fast to it, and repenting. All they needed was to watch and strengthen those who were feeble and dying. Like many churches in our time, there is always a remnant that will keep the doctrine, keep their fire, live up to expectation, and be a true reflection of Christ. In the face of great challenges and persecution, God will always find himself a remnant to keep the faith and their testimony. One thing is sure, He will never leave himself without a witness.

The church of Philadelphia is a picture of the contemporary church that lives up to biblical standards, though it is not immune from trials, struggles, persecution, and abuse. However, the reminder to the faithful church is there will always be an open door that man will not be able to shut. Jesus has established that he's the one with the key of David, symbolic of power and authority, and when he does something it cannot be undone by any inferior power. It is to be admired how the church of Philadelphia maintained its character even when it was weak. Jesus said that even with little strength, it had not denied his name. One can compare this church to many around the world who are faithful although they dwell in hostile provinces where Christianity is not welcomed by the more dominant and radical religious persuasions.

Just a few years ago, there was a leadership and pastoral conference in India designed to accommodate 350 pastors and leaders. This conference was organized and paid for by friends and ministers who wanted to train leaders to reach the indigenous people for the expansion of the kingdom of God. Some of these people experienced exactly what some of the seven churches experienced for their faith. Some were burned alive as a statement to others that Christianity was not welcomed there. In spite of the high level of intolerance and spiritual dogmatism, many were persuaded that their inner conviction of salvation through the redemptive blood of Christ, and it alone, it was worth the risk to develop themselves and gain deeper knowledge of Christ, and then to pass it on to others.

One particular pastor who came to the conference was beaten and jailed; his wife was stoned, knocking out her teeth; his worship leader was shot in the heart; and his church was burned. However, because of his conviction, he traveled for eighteen hours by train to the conference, not sure whether he would make it back alive, or whether he would be able to rebuild his congregation in his community, but he was willing to take the chance. As much as there is some level of hate and religious intolerance among a minority in America, it will never rise to the intensity of what many of the followers of Christ are facing in other parts of the world.

To these people, as he did the Philadelphian church, Christ promised to make those of the synagogue of Satan worship at their feet and would prove to their adversaries how much he loved them.

One might argue that Christ did not keep those people from the hour of temptation, but to the church of Smyrna, Christ told them to be "faithful unto death," (Revelation 2:10) indicating that dying for the cause of Christ is not a disgrace but an honor. They can take your life, but they can't take your crown. As a matter of fact, the Christian's life is hidden with Christ in God and cannot be altered by earthly experiences. Blessed are you when men shall revile and persecute you, and shall say all manner of evil against you for the name of Christ. Suffering for Christ, or with him, is a label one should be proud to wear any time of the day. Peter gives every suffering believer a sense of hope, and pride as he bears the mark of Christ literally for some. "But let none of you suffer as a murderer, or as a thief, or as an evildoer, or as a busybody in other men's matters. Yet if any man suffers as a Christian, let him not be ashamed; but glorify God on this behalf"(1 Peter 4:15-16).

The Laodicean church is the last of the seven churches, which, according to many commentators, truly reflects this current age and stage of the church. When one looks at this church and the status of the church now, even if one wanted to deny that these historical, literal churches, located in the Far East, do not bear any significance to the church over the ages, he or she would be hard-pressed to do so. The picture is clear and undeniably reflected broadly in the church today, especially, if not exclusively, in the so-called mega churches. I do not necessarily want to label mega churches, or make them exclusive, but the comparison could not be more profound. There are some individuals whose actions reflect this church, and their behavior suggests that they need to be recognized and looked up to.

One does not have to look far to see the stark similarities in this day and age. This church had nothing good for Christ to commend, and if Christ the head of the church cannot find something commendable in any church, it is not worthwhile being in the community. A house is not a home unless someone lives in it. Likewise a so called church cannot truly be what it is intended without the occupation of the head who is Christ. It had lost its spiritual standing and was not focused on Christ. It was blinded by the pursuit of wealth, materialistic gain, and self-gratification. The Laodicean church was lukewarm; there was no joy or passion in its worship. It was tepid and insipid, unpalatable, and not relational with Christ, it has no fire or fervor. But it didn't realize it. It had become nothing but an act, and place where people gathered to bask in their own glory and acquisitions.

This church was all about wealth, earthly goods, pride, and self-reliance, as Christ emphasized, "Because thou sayest, I am rich, and increased with goods, and have need of nothing; and knowest not that thou art wretched, and miserable, and poor, and blind, and naked" (Revelation 3:17). It has been a long time since many churches have been heard preaching about the coming of Christ, redemption, regeneration, being born again, and sanctification. These topics have taken the back burner in many churches because they do not make people comfortable in their sins, and demand a change of life and Christlike living. The Laodicean church used the "come as you are" as a stay as you are approach, and did not make provision for a life-changing experience.

> This church is doing the cleanup operation of which the other six Churches did not do. This church is in the business of gathering some of every kind. How is it doing this? Primarily, this Church will do a final sweep of all potential believers and allure them through the avenue of materialism. This church is modifying the gospel of Jesus Christ to "Candy-Coat" it and make it appealing to all. In other words, if you accept Jesus Christ as your Savior, then you can have what you want.[167]

Many churches are experiencing the things that all seven churches experienced, but it is apparent that the Laodicean church is the most significant to the life of the church of this present time. If one searches carefully, he or she will find churches or organizations that are experiencing similar things as the church of Ephesus, Smyrna, Pergamos, Thyatira, Sardis, and Philadelphia. But one does not have to search to find the Laodicean type.

Nothing is wrong with mega churches. Nothing is wrong with a church being able to sustain itself and provide for the needs of its people and community. But something is radically wrong when the church's focus is on wealth, health, prosperity, fame, and popularity,

---

167 RMS Bible Engineering.

rather than on the spiritual life, growth, and maturity of its parishioners. When the focus of the leadership of a church is on personal wealth and popularity, something is inherently wrong.

There are a few examples to consider, all of which have been on television recently. A series on Oxygen TV called *Preachers of LA* gave a glimpse into the lifestyles of some of these renowned preachers, pastors, and bishops. Names will be used here because these have been public events on television, the Internet, and in print.

Bishop Clarence McClendon, a man who not too long ago was a man of the Word and was preaching with an apparent special anointing, has reduced his character to little more than a prosperity preacher. Recently, he was confronted about his consistent prosperity gospel, and his reply was "There is no other kind of gospel." Well, if there is no other gospel, then there is no gospel. This would be in defiance of the apostle Paul's letter to the saints of Galatia.

> I marvel that ye were so soon removed from him that called you into the grace of Christ unto another gospel: Which is not another; but there are some that trouble you, and would pervert the gospel of Christ. But though we, or an angel from heaven, preach any other gospel unto you than that which we have preached unto you, let him be accursed. As we said before, so say we again, if any man preach any other gospel unto you than that ye have received, let him be accursed. (Galatians 1:6–9)

Matthew 24:14 emphatically states, that the gospel of the kingdom shall be preached in all the world for a witness, before the end comes. So if there is no other gospel but one of prosperity: there is a problem in the church, and God help us to figure it out, and figure it out quickly, because while we are striving fatten our pockets with more cash, the people around us both rich and poor are dying in their sins.

Bishop McClendon persuaded his son, who is apparently a secular musician, to become his worship leader, although his son was uncertain how he would be accepted, as he is not a dedicated Christian. His father told him that God had given him the talent for his glory.

One point noted by Bishop McClendon was that, as a young man and a musician growing up, things were not as flexible as they are now, as his father wouldn't allow him to do what he wanted his son to do, by putting him as the worship leader of his church. This proves why the power of the Holy Spirit is virtually absent from many so-called worship services, and they become nothing more than stage performances, and professional acts. We see this cascading more and more among church leaders as they try to match with the other. The ripple effect of that it is becoming like Broadway in our churches, and a competition for who will outdo the other, or have the biggest stage.

Another of the LA preachers, Pastor Wayne Chaney, was justifying getting tattoos, using Revelation 19:16 as his guide. "And he hath on his vesture and on his thigh a name written, KING OF KINGS, AND LORD OF LORDS." This is what the apostle Peter called "wrest," or torture of the Scriptures: "As also in all his epistles, speaking in them of these things; in which are some things hard to be understood, which they that are unlearned and unstable wrest, as they do also the other Scriptures, unto their own destruction" (2 Peter 3:16). This pastor was determined to get his tattoos although his wife tried to discourage him. She suggested to him that some things are not appropriate, especially being leaders of the church, but he would not be deterred by her disapproval.

Pastor Jay Hazlip stated that one-third of the members of his congregation were tattooed, and it appeared that in order to keep them comfortable and not to lose them (maybe because they are big donors), he indulged himself in tattooing so he could look like them. Even his wife had indulged. Why is this important? Jesus said to the Laodicean church that while they were comfortable within, presuming that they wanted nothing, he was outside knocking, pleading for an open door so he could come in. Imagine all the fanfare taking place at some places on a given worship service, pretending to be calling on the name of the Lord, or asserting that the worship and praise were centered on him, and he is saying, hello there on the inside, I am locked out, and I am pleading that someone will let me in. According to Christ's indictment of this church, he said, he was never a part of the celebration on the inside. As a mater for consideration, the activities on the inside were so loud and self centered that no one was able to hear him knocking on the outside.

Not too long ago, two renowned pastors were the center of an investigation: Creflo Dollar and Kenneth Copeland, who Creflo says is his mentor. Creflo Dollar told his congregation that he doesn't want to get to heaven and be broke. He completely missed what sort of wealth is welcomed in heaven. He once said he asked God for ten million dollars to buy an airplane, and God gave him twenty million dollars.

Kenneth Copeland lives (according to a news report) in a fourteen-thousand-square-foot home with his own airport nearby. He has one of the fastest private jets money can buy, says the reporter. When asked about his live-rich lifestyle on the backs of his donors, he replied, "I am living according to what the Bible says." When asked why he had not one but a number of airplanes, his response was sharp and abrupt: "That's none of your business!" Both men, including others, are under investigation by the IRS and Congress and have not been cooperating efficiently, the reports stated.

This is not an indictment or slandering of any of the above-mentioned preachers, as these are all public knowledge broadcasted on Oxygen television channel, but it gives credence to where the church is today as it pertains to the Laodicean church.

This paints a good picture of the letter to the Laodicean church. The reference is not to imply that these men are evil or that their congregations are lost. Rather, they epitomize the very characteristics of the seventh church of Revelation, and a call to recon on what is the most important in the life of the church, and also the life of the pastor.

In one sense, it is hard to blame them because the same people they are coaching into wealth, they took from them what they have to make themselves rich. As mentioned before, many who were considered great preachers have become a shadow of themselves as recently as ten to fifteen years ago because the Spirit's anointing to deliver a life-changing word has often disappeared as they disintegrated in prosperity. Prosperity sermons are not anointed sermons, rather they develop to persuade like motivational speakers. As a result, most of their congregations now focus on what God can give them and not how he wants to change them. People with itching ears, and those who crave materialistic dominance, gravitate to them. It is a good feeling to think that God has earthly wealth for all, and who knows what he has? The problem that arises from such mentality, and false teaching, is that many unfortunate people get angry with God when what they hoped for did not materialize. The Laodicean church was told that wealth not found in Christ is poverty.

But the Bible does say that money answer all things: "A feast is made for laughter, and wine maketh merry: but money answereth all things" (Ecclesiastes 10:19).

Understandably, nothing can get done without money, but when it becomes one's number-one priority, so that it takes the place of a life-changing sermon, or replaces the true worship of Go, something has gone wrong. It is embarrassing to the church in general to have many ministers probed and investigated for fraud, extortion, money laundering, misappropriation, and more. Just one bad apple (especially with a national or international platform) can give the church a black eye and be a main cause why many people do not attend church to get a word from the Lord to change their lives and give them hope beyond the things of this world.

Christ's counsel was that the church buy of him gold tried in fire, that their riches would be counted in heaven, and that they would wear white raiment, symbolic of purity, and be clothed so the shame of their nakedness would not appear. I need not say more about the stark contrast of the Laodicean church portrayed in many of these congregations that are visible to all.

If one notices the approach of the new rush of apostles and prophets, most of what they do, are moneymaking events, where one needs to attend a conference to be told what God has for their future. But they have to pay to receive that word.

Currently, there is a television minister, who only talks about prosperity, sowing, and reaping, called for each person to sow a seed of $273, using some portion of Scripture, chapter and verse, to come to that number. But shortly into his program, he "heard" the Lord say that there was a call for one hundred persons to sow a seed of one thousand dollars for a special abundance in return. This is where the Laodicean church stands out in this time. Sadly, far too many poor and desperate people are blindly and heedlessly falling into the trap of those who extort from them the little God gave them, sometimes because of their own greed, and the deception of those whose goal is no more than grabbing as much as they can for themselves.

Finally, Jesus says, unlike what some may think for the Laodicean church, "I stand at the door and knock." (Revelation 3:20) As mentioned in the study of this church, many people use this verse to speak exclusively to sinners that Christ is knocking at their heart's door. And while it is truth that Jesus through the Holy Spirit knocks at heart of the sinner, it is bad hermeneutics to apply this verse to sinners, while it is clear that the letter was sent to the church and not the lost. It is not a letter for salvation, but one for correction sent to the angel of the church. This verse was given in the letter sent to the church as an indictment against it, that Christ was outside while they were inside saying they wanted nothing. One cannot, however, ignore Christ's desire to see his church change and make him its priority: "As many as I love, I rebuke and chasten: be zealous therefore, and repent" (Revelation 3:19). This shows that as much as the church has lost its focus and has turned to mammon, there is hope. Whoever opens the door, singular or plural, Christ will come in and sit and sup with them, and they with him.

If the church today would take a close look at these seven churches; the letters sent to them; the way they handle their experiences; how Christ rebuked, rewarded, and admonished them; and use them as examples of how the church should conduct itself, the church would have a much greater impact on the world. Just like Solomon who didn't ask the Lord for wealth but for wisdom and understanding to lead his people, and the Lord granted those requests, and afterward gave him wealth, I believe in the same manner if we focus on the lost, the least, and the last, God will supply our needs according to his riches in glory. The Pharisees were offended when they were told to seek first the kingdom of God, and his righteousness, and all things shall be added unto them. But that is the place to begin for the young church, and the not so young ones.

It is with great hope that even with this brief look at these seven churches, the Holy Spirit brought to light some important things, even if only to stimulate an interest to want to know more about them, their significance, and how they reflect the church then and now. May God bless everyone, may he stir the hearts and spirits of all who read this book, and bring about a consciousness that some things of great importance to the life and effect of the church might be missing, or at least slighted or ignored.

Don't be weighed in the balance and found wanting. Keep your eyes open! Learn from history! Set your priorities right! Let God be pleased with what you do. Position the church for Christ's return. It would be a dereliction of duty in ministry, not give priority to souls of the lost, and the lives of those who are struggling to find hope, and to gear our sermons and counsel to that end.

May God bless everyone as you consider these things to do the things that are written in this book. Happy are you if you know these things and do them, is what Jesus told the disciples. Paul says he will take heed to himself lest when he preaches in others, he himself becomes a castaway. We have been admonished!

BIBLIOGRAPHY

Barclay, William. *Letters to the Seven Churches.* Louisville, Ky.: Westminster John Knox Press, 2001.

Cokerham, Larry W. *The Seven Churches:* http:/www.prophecyforum.com/revelation/seven_churches.html (accessed June 7, 2013).

Combs, Jim. *Rainbows from Revelation:* Tribune Publishers, Springfield MO, 1994.

Dake, Finis Jennings. *Dake's Annotated Reference Bible*, Dake Bible Sales, Inc., Lawrenceville, Georgia, 1991.

Deffinbaugh, Bob. https://bible.org/seriespage/1-uniqueness-ephesians-among-epistles (accessed August 18, 2013), 1.

Discover the Book of Revelation, http://www.discoverrevelation.com/Rev_2.html (accessed September 5, 2013).

Easton's Bible Dictionary, http://www.ccel.org/e/easton/ebd/ebd/T0003400.html#T0003462 (accessed September 6, 20013).

Encyclopaedia Britannica. http://www.britannica.com/EBchecked/topic/260307/Hellenistic-Age (accessed September 5, 2013).

Encyclopedia Britannica, http://www.britannica.com/EBchecked/topic/143732/Croesus (accessed August 18, 2013).

English Standard Version, http://www.biblegateway.com/passage/?search=Hebrews%204&version=ESV (accessed September 13, 2013).

Fant, Clyde E., and Reddish, Mitchell G. *A Guide to Biblical Sites in Greece and Turkey*: Oxford University Press, New York 2003.

God's Word Translation, http://www.biblegateway.com/passage/?search=Revelation%203&version=GW (accessed September 13, 2013).

Good News Translation, http://www.biblegateway.com/passage/?search=Leviticus%2010&version=GNT (accessed September 13, 2013).

Grace, George. *The Study of Revelation:* First Bible Baptist Church. Rochester, NY 2010.

Guzik, David. *"Study Guide for Revelation 2."* Enduring Word. Blue Letter Bible. 7 Jul 2006. http://www.blueletterbible.org/Comm/guzik_david/StudyGuide_Rev/Rev_2.cfm (accessed February 12, 2013).

Guzik, David. *"Study Guide for Acts 18."* Enduring Word. Blue Letter Bible. 7 Jul 2006. http://www.blueletterbible.org/Comm/guzik_david/StudyGuide_Act/Act_18.cfm (accessed September 13, 2013).

Henry, Matthew. *Commentary of the Whole Bible:* Vol. VI-Acts to Revelation. Macdonald Publishing Company, McLean, Virginia.

Jamieson, Robert; A.R. Fausset; and David Brown. *"Commentary on Revelation 1."*. Blue Letter Bible. 19 Feb 2000.2013. http://www.blueletterbible.org/Comm/jfb/Rev/Rev_002.cfm (accessed September 13, 2013).

Larkin, Clarence. *The Book of Revelation*: Rev Clarence Larkin Estate, 1919.

Lorie, Peter. Revelation, "St. John the Divine's Prophecies of the Apocalypse and Beyond" Labyrinth Publishing (UK) Ltd, 1994.
McGee, J. Vernon. The Seven Churches of Asia Minor (Part 1). http://www.ldolphin.org/cleanpages/rev02.html (accessed May 7, 2013).

Ramsay, William Mitchell. (2011-11-09). The Letters to the Seven Churches of Asia and Their Place in the Plan of the Apocalypse (With Active Table of Contents) (Kindle Locations 4951-4953). . Kindle Edition.

RMS Bible Engineering, http://www.rmsbibleengineering.com/Page2/Revelation/Page7_Lao.html (accessed June 10, 2013).

Ruckman, Peter S. *The Book of Revelation:* BB Bookstore, Pensacola, FL 1970.

Russsell-Yarde, Peter. Letters to the Seven Churches, (Matters of Faith), Peter Russell-Yarde, 2013.

Saunders, Richard M. *The church at Ephesus.* http://www.rmsbibleengineering.com/Page2/Revelation/Page1_Eph.html (accessed May 7, 2013).

Smith, Chuck. "Revelation 2-3." *The Word for Today*. Blue Letter Bible. 1 Jun 2005.2013. http://www.blueletterbible.org/commentaries/comm_view.cfm?AuthorID=1&contentID=7267&commInfo=25&topic=Revelation (accessed May 7, 2013).

Strong, James. *James Exhaustive Concordance of the Bible.* Nashville Tn.: Abingdon Press, 1962, 1971, 1980, 1986.

The Amplified Bible http://www.biblegateway.com/passage/?search=1+Corinthians+10&version=AmP (accessed September 13, 2013).

The Seven Churches of Revelation: http://www.travelbiblical.com/?p=churches (accessed May 7, 2013).

Unger, Merrill F. *The New Unger's Bible Dictionary*: The Moody Bible Institute of Chicago, 1988.

United Church of God. *The Book of Revelation Revealed:* http://www.ucg.org/booklet/book-revelation-unveiled/ 1/5/2012 (accessed July 20, 2013).

Webb, Brian Thomas. *Strong's Concordance for the iPhone* version 1.5.3, Copyright 2009.

White Wing Publishing House. *The Seven Churches of Asia.* "Know your Bible Series" White Wing Publishing House and Press, Cleveland, Tennessee, 2002.

ABOUT THE AUTHOR

Dr. ORVILLE R. BECKFORD Sr. PhD

Dr. Orville Beckford, Sr. is the Pastor for Grace New Life Center in New Rochelle New York. He has been in ministry for over 40 years. He started pastoring in 1988, and has pastored five churches, both in Jamaica, St. Vincent, and the United States. He served as District Overseer for St. Vincent and St. Lucia, 1992-1995 overseeing ten churches. He is a graduate of Northstar Bible Institute, Rochester, NY (B.D.); Louisiana Baptist University, (B.A., M.A., PhD.)

An active participant and a frequent speaker at numerous church gatherings and community events, Dr. Beckford sets himself apart by his in-depth knowledge of the Word and also his seemingly effortless ability to interact with and humor his audiences. He is an excellent teacher in Discipleship and Homiletics. His career as a Full-time Minister, does not prevent him from actively serving the communities in which he has lived and served, hence the additional responsibilities which come with being a Chaplain, a Notary Public and a Radio Show Host for "A Rhema of Grace," and 95 Degrees with the Doc. do not tire him – if anything, they energize him.

Bishop Beckford not only has had extensive trainings in numerous ministerial and professional disciplines, but has over the years use his gifting in pastoral care, Biblical teaching, discipleship and Christian Counseling to train and develop others. His book – "The Seven Churches of Asia Minor" is just another of the avenues he uses to enlighten readers and Bible Students to be aware of the times, and to help them grow in grace, and in the knowledge of God.

Born in St, Andrew, Jamaica, Dr. Beckford currently resides in Peekskill, New York with his beautiful wife Deana and their two sons, Delton and Jaanai.

Goldia Robinson, PhD

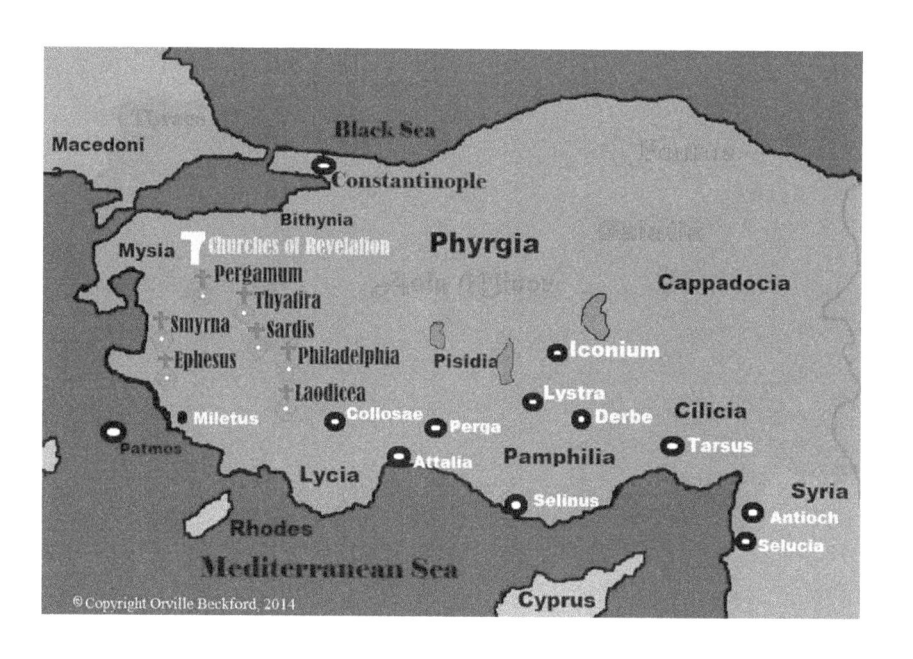

THE SEVEN CHURCHES OF ASIA MINOR

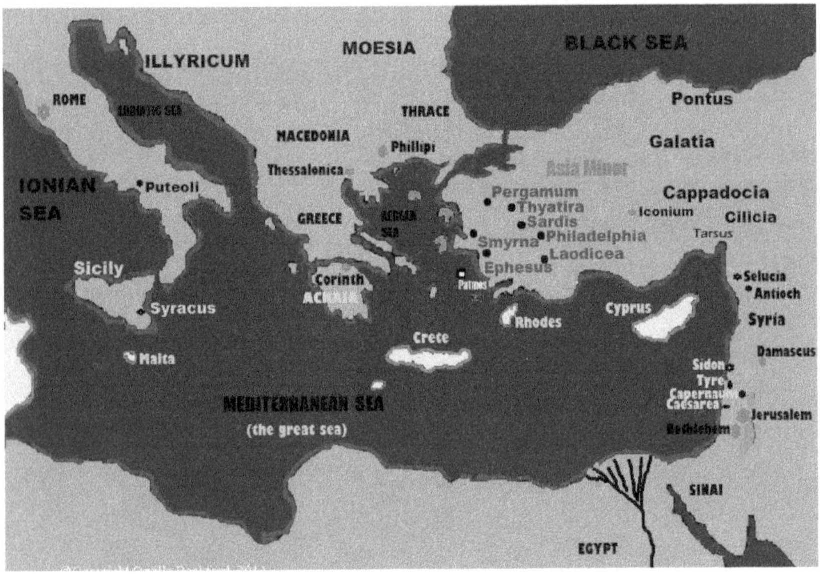
ILLYRICUM
MOESIA
BLACK SEA
ROME
THRACE
Pontus
MACEDONIA
Phillipi
Galatia
Thessalonica
IONIAN SEA
Puteoli
Pergamum
Thyatira
Cappadocia
Iconium
Cilicia
GREECE
Sardis
Smyrna
Philadelphia
Tarsus
Laodicea
Sicily
Ephesus
Selucia
Corinth
Antioch
Syracus
Cyprus
Rhodes
Syria
Crete
Malta
Damascus
Sidon
Tyre
Caesarea
MEDITERRANEAN SEA
Jerusalem
(the great sea)
SINAI
EGYPT

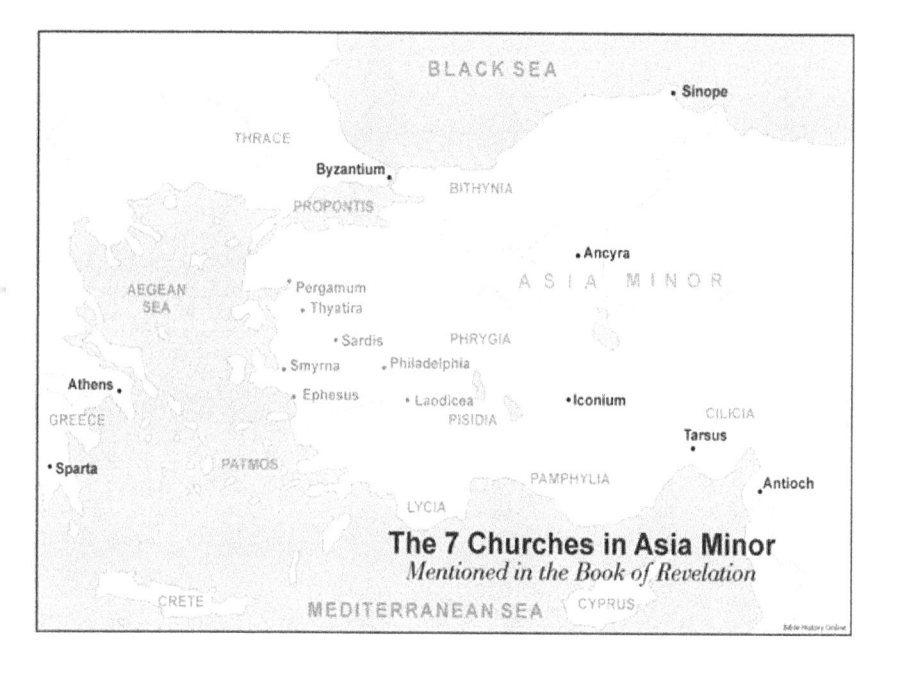

THE SEVEN CHURCHES OF ASIA MINOR

The 7 Churches in Asia Minor
Mentioned in the Book of Revelation

CPSIA information can be obtained
at www.ICGtesting.com
Printed in the USA
BVHW031954180421
605255BV00009B/213

9 781643 985008